CODING FOR KIDS SCRATCH

CODING

FOR KIDS

SCRATCH

LEARN CODING SKILLS, CREATE 10 FUN GAMES, AND MASTER SCRATCH

MATTHEW HIGHLAND

ILLUSTRATIONS BY AMIR ABOU ROUMIÉ

ROCKRIDGE
PRESS

Interior and Cover Designer: Merideth Harte
Art Producer: Sara Feinstein
Editor: Susan Randol
Production Editor: Andrew Yackira
Illustrations: © 2019 Amir Abou Roumié
Author photo courtesy of © C.K. Huntington

ISBN: Print 978-1-64152-245-8 | eBook 978-1-64152-246-5

For Max, Jack, Hiromi, and baby Mahiro

CONTENTS

NOTE FOR PARENTS

Does your child love playing video games? Wouldn't it be nice if you could harness that passion and set your child on a path for future career success in computer programming?

While I was an elementary school teacher in Silicon Valley, I got caught up in the tech culture: so much so that it became difficult for me to focus only on teaching when all around me entrepreneurs were launching billion-dollar companies. I quickly fell in love with the start-up culture, coding, and building websites.

In August 2014, my nine-year-old son said, "Dad, I want to code like you," and that was the lightbulb moment—I needed to build a coding school for kids! And so, Hackingtons was born.

For the past five years, I've taught programming to kids at Hackingtons Code School for Kids. Of all the wonderful experiences I've had, none is as empowering as watching a student use Scratch for the first time. And now I'm happy to deliver this instruction to kids around the world—through this book!

Coding for Kids: Scratch is an easy-to-understand introduction to both programming and video game development using Scratch, a popular online coding environment for kids. Part 1 offers an introduction to programming and the Scratch environment, and part 2 delivers awesome games to build—some inspired by arcade classics. This book will teach your child just how fun, useful, creative, and empowering computer coding can be.

Coding is a blast to learn, especially when you are building video games. For younger children (ages 6–8), I recommend that parents sit with their child and help them navigate the beginning concepts until they are confident enough to use Scratch alone.

Your child will certainly have fun as *Coding for Kids: Scratch* helps them create video games, but the long-term benefits of learning to code are much further-reaching than gaming. And don't be surprised if you, as a parent, suddenly find yourself interested in a career in computer programming!

NOTE FOR PARENTS

INTRODUCTION

Hey, kids! Are you ready to build your own video games?
It's really fun and easy to build video games with Scratch. What is
Scratch? It's a website that allows you to build and launch video games
to the web for the world to play. Yes, all of your friends and family mem-
bers will be able to play the video games you make! And, to make it even
better, you don't even need typing skills! Scratch uses **drag-n-drop**
coding—just click and drag with your computer mouse to build
your games.

Let me introduce myself. I started my career as an elementary school
teacher in Silicon Valley, which is a very famous place for video games
and technology because it is where companies like Atari and Apple
started.

Being around all this exciting technology was contagious—in fact,
I fell in love with coding and building websites myself.

A few years ago, my nine-year-old son said, "Dad, I want to code like
you," and that's when it clicked—
kids want to code, too! All they
need is a place to learn. So I started
Hackingtons Code School for Kids.

For the past five years, I've
taught programming to kids at
Hackingtons Code School for Kids.
It's awesome to watch students
just like you use Scratch for the
first time. I wish I could see your

smile when you launch your first game. Coding is really powerful, and I'm excited to help you learn it!

Are you wondering what you will need to begin this journey? Well, if you have this book, then you're already halfway there. All you need now is a computer or tablet with Internet access.

You may wonder, what is programming? Programming, also known as **coding**, is putting ideas into a form that the computer can understand. Scratch lets you express your ideas using pictures. Other ways for people to program usually involve typing words on a keyboard. But Scratch does the work for you by turning the pictures you create into those words!

There are many computer coding languages in the world. Maybe you have heard of some of them—Python, JavaScript, C++, Java, Ruby—but guess what? Scratch holds a unique place in the world of coding because it was designed by researchers at MIT specifically **for kids to build video games**.

Yes, we are going to build actual video games. But don't worry, we will start with steps as simple as one line of code, then slowly progress towards coding complete games.

Part 1 will teach you the basics of coding in very simple steps. I will also introduce you to the Scratch website and show you how to use it. By the end of part 1, you will have written some very simple video game code.

Part 2 is a collection of easy lessons on how to build different types of video games. The games start out very simple, and I'll introduce lots of fun elements and ideas for you to build on. The best part is, you can make all of the games uniquely your own. You are the game maker, and by the end of part 2, you'll be the game master!

All of the lessons include easy-to-follow step-by-step instructions for programming. Each lesson is illustrated with clear screenshots. My goal is to not only teach you, but to also challenge you and help you show off your creativity and game-building skills.

If you have trouble remembering any of the words or concepts, just check the back of the book for a glossary of coding terms (page 150).

By reading *Coding for Kids: Scratch* and trying the games, you'll embark on a fun adventure that will teach you not only amazing skills for building video games today, but also skills that will serve you well into your future—maybe even as a career!

PART

1

LET'S LEARN TO CODE!

 Before we jump in, there are some basic coding skills and concepts that we should talk about. In part 1, you will learn the basics of coding, how to find your way around the Scratch website, and how to use Scratch drag-n-drop code to build amazing games. Let's get started!

WELCOME TO SCRATCH

Are you excited to build your first video game? I bet you are! Lots of computer programmers fondly remember building their first video games, and you are only steps away from joining the club.

You may be a little nervous, especially if you have never coded before. In chapter 1, I will supercharge your confidence by explaining exactly what programming is and how to get started with Scratch. Trust me, when you see how easy it is to learn Scratch, you'll start to feel like a coding superhero!

WHY SCRATCH?

Do you remember your first word as a child? Probably not. Perhaps you can ask your parents what your first word was. Was it *Mommy*? Or *Daddy*? Or *hello*?

If you were a computer, your first words would likely be *Hello, world*. Huh? Why *Hello, world*? It may sound silly, but it is a tradition for new coders to make the computer say *Hello, world*. Telling the computer to do this is the first program most computer programmers ever run.

So, how do you make a computer say *Hello, world*? First, you need to talk to the computer in its own language. But what language does a computer speak? Computers speak in a language called **binary**, which only has two symbols: 0 and 1. For example, a computer might understand something written like this: 01101000 01101001. (This is the word *hi* in binary.)

Of course, writing 0s and 1s for humans is pretty confusing, so computer engineers and computer scientists created languages that both humans and computers could understand. We call those languages "programming languages."

Scratch is a computer programming language, and it's cool because it looks and reads very much like how you would speak to a friend. With a little practice, you might even start thinking in Scratch code!

When someone is writing a computer program, we say they are *coding*. When you create a video game using Scratch, you are writing a computer program. A program is simply a set of instructions for a computer to follow. Computer programs can be short or very long in length, depending on the video game or application. You might consider the word *coding* to be very similar to the word *writing*. Try using the word *coding* in conversation. Here's an example: "Sorry, Madam President, I'll have to meet with you later. I'm busy coding a video game."

Scratch is just one of many computer coding languages in the world, and new languages are invented all the time. But Scratch has a lot of advantages as a first programming language to learn:

- It's designed for kids.

- It uses drag-n-drop coding (no typing required!).

- You can quickly build and share video games.

- You can see inside the code of other games (see Running a Program, page 7).

- It includes lots of sounds, images, and backdrops.

- It's free to use—no subscription fees or credit cards needed!

Scratch is also super fast for prototyping games. Do you know the word *prototype*? A **prototype** is a quick rough draft of an idea. For example, if you want to build a game about hippos that fart rainbows, you can quickly build a prototype of the game using Scratch. When I say quickly, I mean in about 30 minutes. If I were to code a similar game prototype in a different computer language, like JavaScript, it might take many hours to complete.

Even professional coders love how easily and quickly you can code games with Scratch. It's a language that appeals to all types of coders and game makers, regardless of their age. Are you excited yet? I hope so, because it's time for you to launch the Scratch website and start coding!

USING SCRATCH

This book teaches you how to code in Scratch 3.0, which officially launched on January 2, 2019. Scratch is used all around the world—in more than 150 countries!—and millions of people use it every day. To access the Scratch website, you must be online, using a computer or tablet with a web browser.

ONLINE

The official website for Scratch 3.0 is Scratch.MIT.edu. Scratch requires an up-to-date web browser. The Scratch team recommends using Chrome, Firefox, or Safari. Internet Explorer is not currently supported for Scratch 3.0.

OFFLINE

There is an offline version of Scratch (one you can use without being connected to the Internet) available for download at Scratch.MIT.edu/download. Currently, the offline version will only work on PC or Mac computers. At the time of publication of this book, the offline version is still in development, and many features, such as sharing *projects* to the web, are not yet available.

BEFORE YOU BEGIN

Before starting with Scratch, I recommend that you register for a free account and log in. Scratch only requires a parent or guardian's e-mail address to create an account, and you will have instant access to your account. Just remind your adult to check their e-mail inbox and accept Scratch's usage terms; otherwise, you will not be able to share your finished games on the web. If you (or your parents) don't see the e-mail in the inbox, check the spam folder.

Scratch automatically saves your projects and keeps a portfolio of all your games. It's a really nice feature, and it allows you to log in on any computer and quickly find the Scratch project you want to work on.

Here are other Scratch basics you need to know before you start coding.

RUNNING A PROGRAM

Scratch games are designed to start and stop just like a car race. You will click the *green flag* icon to start a game and click the *red stop sign* icon to stop.

A great place to see Scratch games in action is on the Scratch homepage (Scratch.MIT.edu). Scratch highlights popular games made by other kids, and you can click on the games and try them out. You can even click the SEE INSIDE button in the upper right-hand corner of each project and check out the code written by the author!

FINDING AND FIXING BUGS

Every computer programmer wants their game to work perfectly. But it is perfectly normal for a game to have some unexpected issues. Whenever something happens in a game that wasn't expected, we call these errors **bugs**. But coders don't try to kill bugs with bug spray; we try to fix the errors by replacing them with better code.

7

Just remember, even the best coders in the world deal with bugs in their code. Bugs are not a bad thing. They're just part of the process of building video games! You'll get better at coding by solving those unexpected issues and fixing bugs.

SAVING YOUR WORK

My dog ate my code! Okay, that excuse probably won't work with Scratch, because as long as you are logged into your Scratch account, it autosaves. Of course, it's best to name your project so you can find it when you want it. And, if you have a really special project, you can download the project to your computer by selecting *File* and then *Save to your computer.*

But making backups of your games is usually not necessary, as Scratch continually saves your code to your online portfolio. Don't believe me? Simply click on your username in the menu (upper right-hand corner of the page) and select *My Stuff.* And presto! Your games will all be listed there—well, not if you haven't coded anything yet!

KEYBOARD CONTROL

Video games are fun because the player is in complete control. Most games use a game controller, a touch-sensitive screen, a joystick, the arrow keys, a mouse, or the keys W, A, S, and D to move the sprites on the screen. Scratch allows you to build games with any of these user controls, but it's unlikely you'll have a joystick.

Scratch 3.0 is a big improvement over the previous version because it allows you to build and play Scratch games on a tablet. Since tablets do not have physical keyboards, you may find that some games that worked well on a computer might not work as well on a tablet.

All of the example games in part 2 of this book are designed to work on both tablets and computers. It's not always easy to build games that work perfectly on both tablets and computers, but I think it's a fun challenge. I'll give you some really easy tips for how to make your games mobile-friendly. What is mobile-friendly? It means the game works on phones and tablets. Basically, mobile means anything that doesn't have a physical keyboard.

CODE COMPLETE!

Well done—you're on your way! You now know that:

- Scratch is fun for all abilities of coders, partly because it makes building games super fast compared with other coding languages.

- Scratch can be accessed by any online computer at Scratch.MIT.edu.

- Problems or errors in your coding are called *bugs*.

- Scratch 3.0 allows you to build games for computers and touch-screen tablets.

Now, let's go take a behind-the-scenes tour of the Scratch editor (the tool in Scratch that you use for making your code)!

THE SCRATCH EDITOR

The Scratch homepage is filled with example games and highlighted projects from other students. Take some time to try other games, look at the code (by clicking the SEE INSIDE button), and get a feel for what is possible with Scratch. It's really cool to have your game featured on the Scratch homepage. If you receive this great honor, your game is truly special!

Playing other kids' games is fun and a great way to find inspiration for your own ideas. But, of course, building games is even better.

In this chapter, I will introduce the Scratch editor, where you will begin to explore the Scratch coding environment. I'll explain very simply how to navigate the Scratch editor, and what the different tools can do.

The Scratch editor is all about building games with drag-n-drop code. It might look like a lot at first, but as I explain all the parts in this chapter, you will see how simple it really is.

TO GET STARTED

To access the Scratch editor from the Scratch homepage, simply click the CREATE button in the top left-hand corner. This will open the Scratch editor on the left side of the screen and display a blank project page on the right side of the screen. The blank project page will have an orange cat character on a white background. We'll call this blank project page the **stage**. (If you see a pop-up tutorial window over the lower part of the code area, just click on the "x" in the upper right-hand corner of that window to close it.)

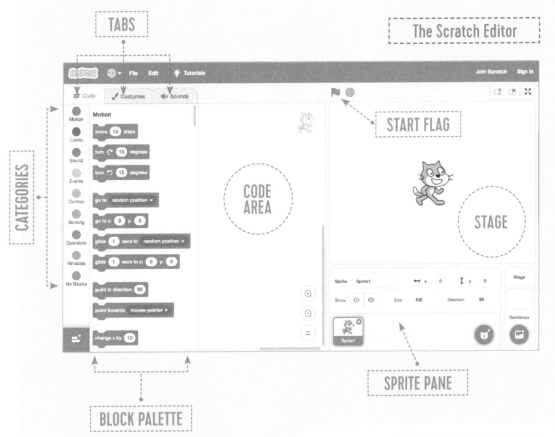

TABS

The Scratch Editor

CATEGORIES

START FLAG

CODE AREA

STAGE

SPRITE PANE

BLOCK PALETTE

THE SCRATCH EDITOR

STARTING WITH SPRITES

The characters in your game are called **sprites**. The most famous Scratch sprite is the orange cat. When you start a new game, the only sprite on the stage is the orange cat.

Below the stage, you will see the sprite pane. You'll notice the orange cat appears in the sprite pane with the name "Sprite1" by default. If you look above the sprite pane, you'll see information about the sprite, including its name, location, visibility, size, and direction.

You can add more sprites to your game by adding them to the sprite pane. Find the blue button that has a white cat's head with a plus symbol (+) next to it. This is the CHOOSE A SPRITE button. Place your mouse pointer on the CHOOSE A SPRITE button. A green label will pop up if you don't click it, like in the picture. If you click it, it will take you to the sprite **library**. To go back to the editor, click the BACK button in the upper left-hand corner of the window.

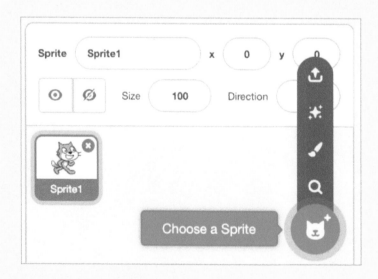

CODING FOR KIDS SCRATCH

In the sprite pane, there is a white space and a blue space. In the blue space, look for the small image with the orange cat on it. This is the sprite thumbnail. You will click this thumbnail to select a specific sprite and see its Code, Sounds, and Costumes tabs. You can delete a sprite by clicking the X symbol in the upper right-hand corner of the sprite thumbnail.

SPRITE LIBRARY

You can add as many sprites as you would like to your game, or just have one. It's a lot of fun to look in the sprite library and check out the selection.

To view the sprite library, click on the CHOOSE A SPRITE button (the blue cat button). To view the sprite library using a touchscreen tablet, press and hold the CHOOSE A SPRITE button until the library appears.

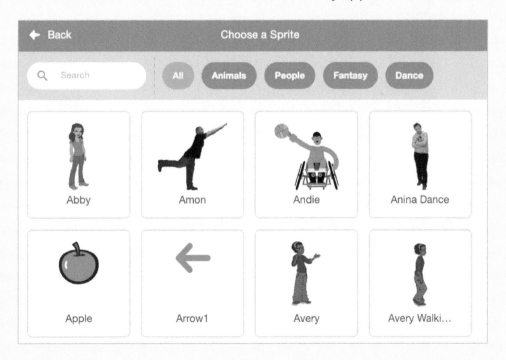

THE SCRATCH EDITOR

There are hundreds of sprites in the library. While you're in the library, you can also quickly find one you want by using the search bar in the top-left corner. And guess what else? If you don't find the sprite you need in the library, you can always decide to draw your own. We'll talk more about the Paint Editor on page 54.

CREATING SCRIPTS

The blank space in the center of the Scratch editor is known as the "code area" (see the following screenshot). This is where you will drag-n-drop code blocks to build your video game.

CODING FOR KIDS SCRATCH

Do you see those blue, rectangular-looking code *blocks* on the left side of the screen? When you attach those blocks of code together, they are called *scripts*. We call them scripts because they work just like movie or play scripts, meaning they tell actors (or sprites) what to do. In movies, the actors read their scripts and follow the directions. In video game programming, the sprites follow the instructions of the coding scripts.

Try dragging a code block from the left-side block palette to the code area. Use the scroll bar on the right-hand side of the block palette to scroll down and see more code blocks that are not initially visible. Pick a code block or two. I picked the yellow WHEN GREEN FLAG CLICKED block and the blue MOVE 10 STEPS block. Click and hold with your mouse button, drag the code block into the code area, and release the mouse button. If you are on a tablet, simply press and hold to drag the code blocks into the code area.

DRAG-N-DROP

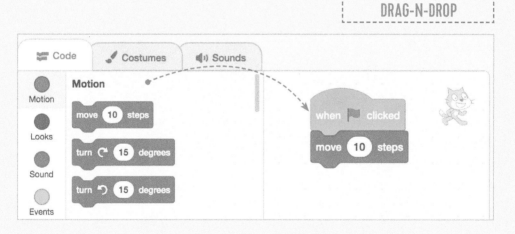

To delete or remove a code block from the code area, simply drag the code block back to the left side of the screen. You can also delete a code block by right-clicking with a mouse on a computer or by doing a press-and-hold with your finger on a tablet. This will pop open a menu to reveal the "Delete Block" option.

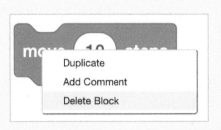

Each sprite in your game has its very own script, so you can only see the code area for the sprite that is currently selected. You can toggle (switch) the code area view by clicking on a different sprite in the sprite pane. Remember, you need to code scripts for every sprite individually. That means that if you have a dog sprite and a cat sprite in your game, they will each have their own code areas.

THE STAGE

The stage is where your sprites perform their actions as written in your scripts. You'll use the stage area to test how your video game looks and acts, and to search for bugs in your code. Most importantly, the stage is what the player will see when they play your video game.

At the top of the stage is the *green flag* icon. You will use this to start games. Next to the green flag is the *red stop sign* icon. You can click this to end a game.

The stage is measured in units, called Scratch units. The stage is 480 units wide and 360 units high.

I'm sure you are wondering, "What is a Scratch unit?" It is a very small distance, about the width of the lowercase letter L (l). Your computer

CODING FOR KIDS SCRATCH

will automatically increase the size depending on your monitor's screen size. This is sort of like what happens to words written on a deflated balloon that is then blown up. The words on the balloon still look the same, but they are stretched out and much larger.

Although the actual measurement of the stage is 480 by 360 units, we use a special way of describing height and width of the stage, starting from zero in the center.

When you add a new sprite to your game, it will appear at position (x:0, y:0). This is the exact center of the stage.

When you move a sprite on the stage, the sprite's (x, y) position changes.

If you move a sprite left, starting from the center, the x position will get smaller until it reaches -240 (negative 240). If you move to the right, it will get larger until the x value reaches 240.

If you move the sprite up or down, the y position will change. If the sprite moves up from the center, the y position will increase up to 180. If the sprite moves down from the center, the y position will decrease, all the way down to -180.

The top-right corner of the stage is (x:240, y:180).

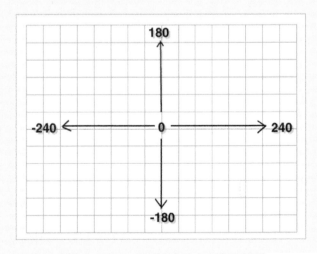

You can always see a sprite's exact position listed below the stage, in the sprite's information window. Whichever sprite is currently selected will have its exact position displayed there.

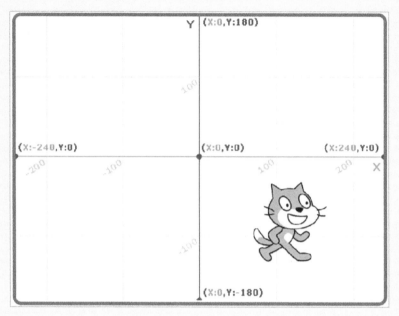

This example shows the cat at position (x:118, y:-81). Don't stress too much about learning the (x, y) positioning system if you are new to this kind of graphing. All you really need to know as a beginner is how to move a sprite, and we'll cover that in the next chapter. (And note that I added the labels to the x and y axes and the coordinates in the four quadrants to the screenshot to make it easier to understand. You won't see these lines or numbers in the stage when you're in Scratch.)

BLOCK PALETTE

If this is your first time using Scratch 3.0, you may be a little distracted by all the colorful categories on the far left-hand side of the screen. These *block categories* organize the code blocks that are used to build scripts. Each code block performs a specific task or function, and you will need to become familiar with the location of each block. To make the job of hunting for code blocks much simpler, they are color coded and quickly searchable by clicking the colorful category buttons on the left side of the menu.

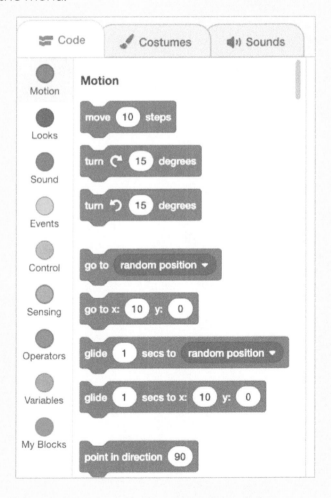

Yes, there are a lot of different code blocks in Scratch. And if you're nervous about all this information, don't fear!

First, we're going to focus on the most important code blocks in this book. You won't have to learn them all just yet.

Second, all the code blocks are color-coded, which makes them easier to identify and understand.

Let's take a quick look at the basic code blocks you will need to jump-start your Scratch coding skills.

MOTION (BLUE)

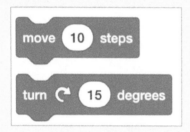

Motion blocks are the action steps of a video game. You can make the sprite turn, move, glide, or go to a random position.

LOOKS (PURPLE)

Looks blocks change a sprite's appearance. You can make it do things like change size, hide/show, change costumes, and change color through lots of wild color effects.

SOUND (PINK)

Sound blocks allow sprites to play music and make sound effects, and you can even record your own sounds!

EVENT (YELLOW)

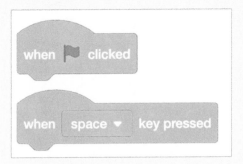

Event blocks control when a script will ***run***. All code blocks require an Event block attached at the beginning. They are like the green starting flag in a race. In fact, there is a green starting flag Event block!

CONTROL (ORANGE)

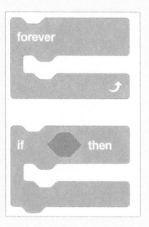

Control blocks are shaped like the letter C because they wrap around other blocks. After being wrapped by a Control block, the contained code will only run according to the "rules" of the control block. For example, FOREVER blocks will repeat all of the code placed inside of them, over and over again. IF-THEN blocks will only run code if certain conditions are TRUE, such as "if" the cat touches the mouse.

VARIABLES (DARK ORANGE)

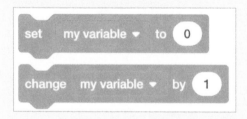

Variables blocks allow you to create places to store lives, points, and other meaningful values in a game. You can create a **variable** with any name, and then give it a value. For example, I can make a variable called "hippo farts" and give it a value of 0. These "hippo farts" are the points in a game. As you play, you collect "hippo farts." You can program your game to go up to 5 points, or 10, or even a million! Oh my! That's disgusting! Why would you ever want a million hippo farts? The point is, you can call the variable anything you want—points, goals, or yes, even hippo farts. And as you can see from the picture, the CHANGE MY VARIABLE BY block will allow you to make each point worth 1 or 5 or 10 or any amount.

CODE COMPLETE!

Is your brain full of new information? Think about all you've learned in this chapter! You now know:

- The *Scratch editor* is where you will build games. You can access it by clicking the CREATE button from the Scratch homepage at Scratch.MIT.edu.

- Characters in video games are called *sprites.*

- The Scratch *sprite library* has loads of sprites to choose from.

- Code blocks are *drag-n-dropped* to the code area to create coding scripts.

- The *stage* is what the player will see when they play your video game.

- A sprite's position on the stage is based on the coordinate graphing system, with (x:0, y:0) being the center and (x:240, y:180) being the top-right corner of the stage.

- You can use the colored *block categories* on the left side of the Scratch editor to explore the different code blocks.

- *Code blocks* are organized by color for easy reference, and you now know what each color is used for.

Now that you know your way around the sprite window, let's write and run some scripts!

BUILDING & RUNNING A SCRIPT

Now that you've learned the basic Scratch tools, you can use them to create scripts—and then run those scripts to create and play games!

YOUR FIRST SCRIPT

I like to think of coding as art. When you connect Scratch code blocks together, you are creating something special and unique. There are no rules for coding video games. Sure, there are easier and harder ways to get things done, but the end result is all that really matters. The world will not judge you by your code, but by how fun your game is. So don't be afraid to take risks and have fun with this chapter. And remember, the more you practice, the better your coding skills will become!

MAKE YOUR SPRITE MOVE (STEPS)

Let's begin your coding journey with Motion blocks. Our first goal will be to move the Scratch cat across the stage.

To begin, try dragging the MOVE 10 STEPS block into the code area.

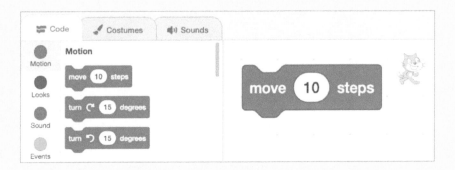

Adding a single movement block into the code area will not suddenly make your sprite move. Code blocks require an Event block to trigger (activate) the code. There are a few different Event blocks we could use, such as the WHEN GREEN FLAG CLICKED block or the WHEN THIS SPRITE CLICKED block. For this example, I suggest attaching a WHEN SPACE KEY PRESSED block, so we'll drag this Event block into the code area.

When blocks of code are snapped together, they form scripts. Scripts can be as small as two blocks connected together (as in our example), or they can be very long and made of many blocks. When the script successfully runs in Scratch, we'll see the entire collection of blocks highlight yellow (it looks like they "glow").

Congratulations, you created your first script! Now, let's test it out by pressing the space key and watching the cat move 10 steps. Yay! You're ready to move on!

MOVING UP, DOWN, LEFT, AND RIGHT

The MOVE 10 STEPS block will move the cat in the direction he is already facing. But, as the game builder, you'll want to have full control over the movement of your sprites.

To move in all directions, we need to understand how the x and y positions work.

The x position controls the left-right position of the sprite. To move the cat left or right, you change the x position. Easy, right?

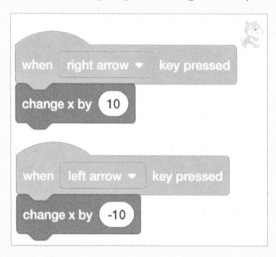

In the screenshot, you can see that I've added the WHEN SPACE KEY PRESSED block. If you click on the word "space," a drop-down menu will pop up. Using the drop-down menu, I selected "right arrow," so now the whole block says WHEN RIGHT ARROW KEY PRESSED. I did the same thing to make the WHEN LEFT ARROW KEY PRESSED block. Then I dragged the CHANGE X BY block below each one, and changed the numbers. Pro tip: Because these two code scripts are almost identical, rather than drag-n-drop to build the second script, I simply duplicated the first script by right-clicking with the mouse pointer and then selecting Duplicate from the menu that pops up.

And, yes, you guessed it: The y position controls the up-down position of the sprite. To move the cat up or down, you'll change the y position.

We'll do the same thing for the y direction, but we'll use the CHANGE Y BY block instead. Remember to add a minus sign (-) to make negative numbers!

You can now use your up, down, left, and right arrow keys to move the sprite around. Go ahead, give it a try!

DIRECTION AND ROTATION

The cat now moves around the stage, but he always points in the same direction. We want to be able to make him go the other way, and we can fix this with the POINT IN DIRECTION block.

You can control the direction a sprite is facing by using the POINT IN DIRECTION block. You can pick the direction you want to program in one of two ways. First, you can type the number (positive or negative, remember?) in the block. Second, you can use the direction-pointer that

27

pops up from the drop-down menu when you click on the white circle with a number in it on the block—simply move the arrow to face the correct direction.

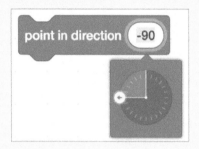
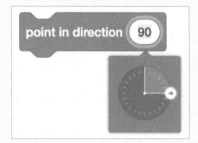

As you adjust the number, the direction-pointer image changes to match. And if you change the direction-pointer image, the number will change to match. In the screenshot, you can see see the difference between the left and right direction.

Let's add the POINT IN DIRECTION block to our movement script for when the left arrow key is pressed and set the value to -90. Now press the left arrow key to run your script.

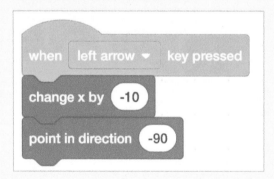

Surprise! Did you see the cat flip upside down? I bet you didn't expect that! Sprites always rotate upside down when you point them to the left, unless you tell them not to. So how do we tell them not to rotate? By snapping the SET ROTATION STYLE block onto the "when left arrow key pressed" block. This is already set to left-right to tell the sprite not to rotate.

POSITION OF YOUR SPRITE

Understanding where your sprites are on the stage is very important. If you are not familiar with (x, y) coordinate graphing, this might be a little tricky to understand at first. But don't worry, you'll quickly get the hang of it with some practice.

Remember, the center of the Scratch stage is at (x:0, y:0). If you want a sprite to appear at the center of the stage at the beginning of the game, then you will create a starting script with these exact coordinates as shown:

I start a lot of my games with the GO TO block. The GO TO block will make a sprite suddenly pop from one location to another on the stage. But if you want to see the sprite actually move across the stage, then you'll want to use the GLIDE block.

Let's use the GLIDE block to show where different locations (coordinates) are on the Scratch stage. Please note: I am showing four complete examples, and you'll need to test them one at a time.

First, let's explore the x position value inside the GLIDE block, which changes the left-right movement of the sprite.

Add the GLIDE block into the code area. The block will already be set to 1 second, and we'll leave it. This means that the sprite will complete the glide movement in 1 second. If we changed it to 2 seconds, the sprite would the take 2 seconds to complete the glide movement.

When the x value is -240, the cat will move to the farthest left side of the stage.

When the x value is 240, the cat will move to the farthest right side of the stage.

Now let's practice changing the y value. The y value controls the up-down location of a sprite.

When the y value is 180, the cat will move to the very top of the stage.

CODING FOR KIDS SCRATCH

When the y value is -180, the cat will move to the very bottom of the stage.

ANIMATION

Animating your sprites in Scratch games adds a professional touch to your games, and it's very easy to do.

Let's animate the Scratch cat. First, we need to check if the Scratch cat has multiple costumes. In Scratch, a **costume** is an alternate image that can be used to switch the appearance of a sprite. Sprites added from the sprite library may or may not have multiple costumes already included. You can view a sprite's costumes by clicking the "costumes" tab at the top of the screen. Each sprite will have a different number of costume options. Click on the COSTUMES tab at the top of the screen. And yes, we are in luck! The cat has two costumes, named "costume1" and "costume2."

BUILDING & RUNNING A SCRIPT

To create *animation*, we switch very quickly between these two costumes.

To switch a sprite's costume, you can use the NEXT COSTUME block. The NEXT COSTUME block is found in the purple Looks menu. (Be sure to switch back to the Code tab in order to see the code blocks.) Let's practice animating the cat by changing the costume when the space key is pressed.

Now, press the space key a few times. Hey, look—he's walking in place!

But costumes aren't just about animation. You can also use costumes to paint or alter your sprite. We'll explore this in chapter 4.

REPEAT AND FOREVER LOOPS

Our animation code works, but pressing the space bar over and over is kind of annoying. Isn't there a better way? Yes, actually there is! We can use loops.

Loops are found in the Control block menu, and they allow you to easily repeat coding scripts.

The most common types of loops are REPEAT loops and FOREVER loops.

Let's practice each type of loop, using our animation as an example. And let's change it up. Instead of using the WHEN SPACE PRESSED key, let's start our code with the WHEN GREEN FLAG CLICKED key.

The following code shows the REPEAT block. You can adjust the number of repeats by changing the number in white (also known as the *parameter*). Give it a try. Then try increasing the parameter from 10 to 100—or even more if you dare!

Now let's compare it with the FOREVER loop. But let me warn you, once you start a forever loop, there is no going back! Okay, I'm just kidding—you can always stop it by clicking the red stop sign at the top of the stage.

Try it. Did you notice that both the repeat and forever loops are incredibly fast? It looks like the cat is running a million miles an hour! Let's learn how to slow down a loop by using a WAIT block.

WAIT

The computer sometimes runs loops so fast that we can barely see what is happening. And this can cause bugs in our code. In part 2 of this book, you'll see me use WAIT blocks to slow down loops. But why wait? Let's try it out now!

The WAIT 1 SECOND block can be adjusted by changing the parameter (1 second). In Scratch, you cannot write fractions—only decimals—so I will use the decimal 0.3 to represent a number between 0 and 1.

You'll see me use 0.3 as the parameter for my WAIT blocks. I like that number for animations. It seems to work well because it's not too fast or too slow.

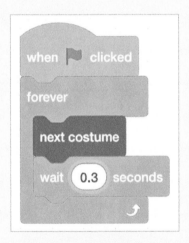

Try running this script. Better, right?

CODE COMPLETE!

You've learned even more tools to help you code now. In this chapter, you learned:

- To move a sprite left and right, you change the x position.

- To move a sprite up and down, you change the y position.

- The center of the stage is at (x:0, y:0).

- To keep a sprite from rotating upside down, you can use the SET ROTATION STYLE block.

- Animations are created by switching costumes using the NEXT COSTUME block.

- *Loops* are found in the Control block menu and they allow code to repeat itself very quickly.

- WAIT blocks help slow down a loop.

Now that we've learned some basic tricks, we'll explore how you can add your own personal touches to make your code unique and fun!

MAKE YOUR GAME FUN!

One of the best parts of coding is figuring out what you want your game to do and what you want it to look like. Here are some things to consider when you decide to make a game.

START WITH A GOAL

What do you want to accomplish in your game? You can create silly games, action games, skill games, or even annoying games. But, please, not *too* annoying!

When people play a game, they expect the game to have a *goal*. In other words, they want to "win" the game. Keep that in mind when you start coding your first game.

I ask four important questions when I create a game:

1. Who is the main character?
2. What can the main character do?
3. Does anyone or anything try to stop the main character from reaching the goal?
4. What happens when the main character reaches their goal?

Your answers will affect what you decide to put in your game.

CHOOSE A BACKDROP

Where will your game begin? The moon? A swimming pool? I often select a **backdrop** for my game to give me inspiration for my coding. The backdrop library is located on the lower-right side of the Sprite menu. The choices are endless—you can either select a backdrop from the library or paint your own (see the Paint Editor section on page 54).

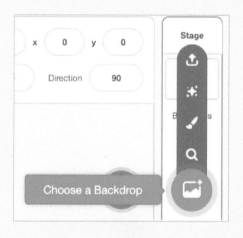

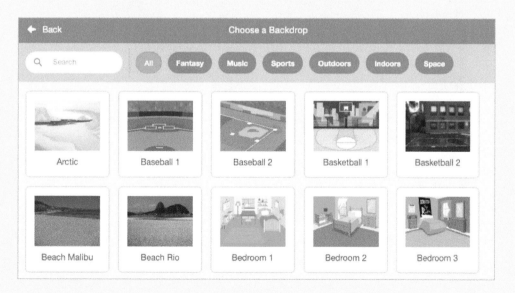

ADDING SOUNDS

Every sprite in Scratch has access to the *sound library*. Yes, you can make your cat say "Moo" or make cartoon noises. Most sprites come preloaded with a single sound in the SOUNDS tab. For example, the cat comes with the sound "Meow." To access the sound library, first click the SOUNDS tab. You can access the Sound Library by clicking the blue and white speaker icon located at the bottom left of the editor—but remember, this icon is only visible when you are in the SOUNDS tab.

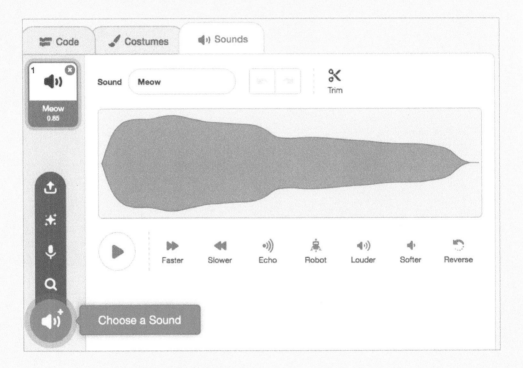

   The sound library is pretty amazing, with endless (and some very funny) possibilities and inspiration for your games. After you've clicked CHOOSE A SOUND, try hovering your mouse over the sounds to hear a sample. To add the sound to your code, simply click to select that sound.

After you have selected the sound, it should now show as available in the SOUNDS tab of your sprite.

Next, switch tabs to the CODE tab, and select the Sounds block menu (purple).

IF-THEN

If I were to choose any type of code block and say, "This is the most important," it would definitely be the IF-THEN block. If I were you, I'd print out a poster of the IF-THEN block and hang it on the wall. I'm just kidding! But it is really important. IF-THEN blocks let us make something happen only in certain situations.

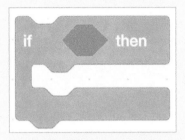

IF-THEN blocks are "C" shaped blocks that wrap around other code blocks and only run codes when specific conditions are TRUE. Wait! What is the condition? Perhaps I should slow down and explain.

Do your parents ever tell you, "If you finish your homework, then you can play video games?"

The condition is, "Did you finish your homework?" And that condition can only have two possible values: TRUE or FALSE.

Therefore, if you finished your homework, you get to play video games. But what if you didn't finish your homework? Well, in that case it would be FALSE, and nothing would happen.

That's how an IF-THEN block works. It is checking if a condition is true, and then running code.

THE TRUE/FALSE CONDITION

Remember when we talked about how computers use the binary language of 1s and 0s? Computers read these 1s and 0s as meaning "yes"/"no" or "on"/"off" or "TRUE"/"FALSE." Do you see the pattern? Computer programs can be extremely complex, but at their core, computers can really only understand 0s and 1s. Because of this, you must build programs that have a "yes"/"no" or "TRUE"/"FALSE" pattern. To do this, we rely on IF-THEN blocks.

IF-THEN blocks require conditions that have values of either TRUE or FALSE.

There are two types of code blocks that will work as conditionals: Sensing blocks and Operators blocks.

You'll always be able to identify TRUE/FALSE condition blocks by looking at the shape. If the left and right sides of the block are pointed, then it is a TRUE/FALSE condition block.

First, let's look at one of the TRUE/FALSE condition blocks we'll use most often, the TOUCHING block. There are two types of "'touching" blocks: one for touching another sprite, and the other for touching a color. Let's closely examine the "touching mouse-pointer" condition block. This block is most commonly used to sense whether one sprite is touching another sprite. You can determine what you are checking for by selecting the drop-down options. As you add additional sprites to your game, they will be included in the touching drop-down. For my example, I added the "Mouse1" sprite to my game, and now it appears as an option for the cat to touch.

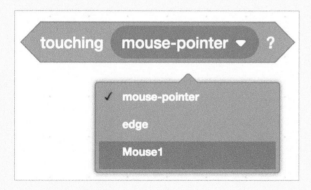

The other most commonly used condition block is a Sensing block called "touching color." To adjust the color the block is sensing, simply click on the color button, and a color palette will be revealed below.

Hint: To select a specific color from your game, be sure to use the color picker at the bottom of the menu. For example, if you want to select the color of the orange cat, click on the color picker and then click on the cat. This will change the color circle to the same color as the cat, or at least the part of the cat that you clicked on.

Now, let's take a look at some TRUE/FALSE condition blocks from the Operators menu.

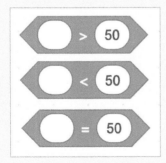

In order to use the operators, you will need to fill in the parameters (white ovals).

Let's try a very simple example:

In the above example, I typed the number 100 into the empty parameter. The preferred technique would be to insert a value that can change during game play. These blocks are known as "reporters" and are taught on page 50.

Ask yourself, is 100 greater than 50? The answer is yes, so this conditional block has the value of TRUE. If we changed the parameter (the value we put in the white space) to 20, this conditional block would have a value of FALSE, because 20 is not greater than 50.

BUILDING A COMPLETE IF-THEN BLOCK

Now that you understand a little bit of how an IF-THEN block works, let's see it in action!

First, we need two volunteers from the audience. Okay, how about the cat sprite and mouse sprite? Come on up! (Go back to page 12 if you need a reminder of how to add a new sprite.)

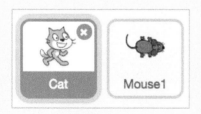

Now let's get to know our two guests. Cat, if you touch a mouse, what happens?

I'm guessing that you are very pleased with yourself, and say "Meow."

43

Let's demonstrate a complete IF-THEN statement in action. But before we begin, I need to be clear about who is touching the mouse. Yes, it is the cat who will be touching the mouse, so we need to be sure to select the cat from the sprite pane and add the script to the Code Area for the cat.

Now, let's look at the basic structure when creating an IF-THEN block of code.

First, we build the basic IF-THEN block, inserting our condition of "touching Mouse1." Then we add code inside the IF-THEN block, which will run only if the condition is TRUE.

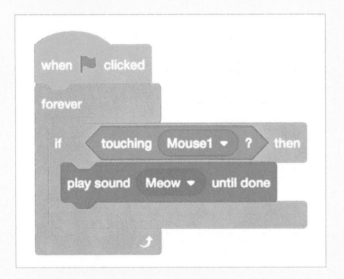

Do you see that I wrapped a FOREVER loop around the IF-THEN block? This is because I want to continually check if the cat and mouse are touching. If I don't wrap it in a FOREVER loop, the script will only run a single time, when the green flag is clicked.

A very important concept in programming is that computers follow instructions exactly. Computers never guess—they just run code in the order that it is written. Why is this important? Because new Scratch programmers often forget to wrap IF-THEN blocks inside of FOREVER loops.

And if you want to always be checking if something happened, you must wrap the IF-THEN block inside a FOREVER loop.

Is there ever a situation where an IF-THEN block is not wrapped in a FOREVER loop? Yes—if the TRUE/FALSE condition is already determined when the event block triggers, it would not require a FOREVER loop; however, the IF-THEN block would only run a single time. And this technique would only be for more advanced Scratch coders.

WAIT UNTIL

Did the if-then lesson seem a little complicated? Never fear, the WAIT UNTIL block is super easy!

The WAIT UNTIL block works just like an IF-THEN block, but it doesn't require the FOREVER loop. The downside is that it only works one time. In the following example, the script will actually wait until the cat is touching the mouse before running the code.

Give it a try. Easy, right?

VARIABLES

I'm curious, how old are you? Are you 6, 7, 8, 9, 10, or perhaps 72 years old? Will you be the same age forever? Hopefully not! Age is a **variable** in your life. A variable has a value, but like your age, that value can change over time.

In coding, we create variables to hold values that might change in our game. Some examples are points, lives, or high score.

In Scratch, you can create and modify variables using the Variables block menu.

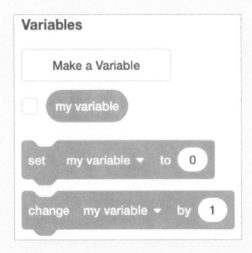

Scratch comes with one variable already made and ready to use. It is the MY VARIABLE block. We'll use this one to learn how variables work and then later on, we'll make our own variables!

A variable does not have a value until you give it one. So let's set the value to zero in our code area.

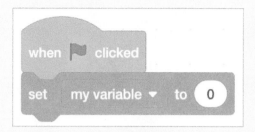

Oh, I almost forgot! You probably would like to see what a variable looks like on the stage, wouldn't you? Click on the checkbox next to the variable's name, and it will appear in the top-left corner of the stage.

Now, let's learn how to change a variable. Let's use our wonderful volunteers, Cat and Mouse.

Remember the if-then code we made where if the cat touches the mouse, then the cat will make a "Meow" sound? Let's use the same code block, but instead of making a sound, let's increase the variable's value.

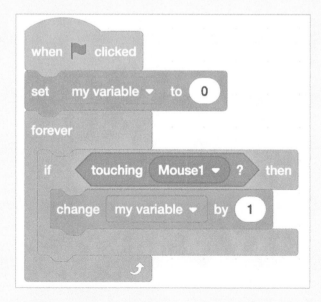

47

Now I must give you a little warning: The code example will work, but as long as the cat is touching the mouse, the variable will keep increasing. And not slowly, but very, very quickly. So when you use this type of script, be aware that you need to move or hide the mouse sprite immediately after the variable changes. Don't worry too much about this for now, as I will demonstrate this many times in part 2.

For all of the example games in this book, we will primarily use variables to keep the score. Let's start building our own!

KEEPING SCORE

Now that we've seen a variable in action, let's build our own and learn how to keep score in our games. First, we need to make a variable by selecting the MAKE A VARIABLE button in the Variables menu.

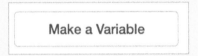

Next, we name it either "Score" or "Points." Actually, you can name a variable anything you want—get creative!

CODING FOR KIDS SCRATCH

Click "For all sprites." The "For this sprite only" button is used more in more difficult coding.

After you have created a variable, it will be available to use in the Variables code menu. Use the drop-down in the "change my variable by 1" block to select your new variable.

To increase the score during a game, you will need either an *Event* or conditional (IF-THEN) block that triggers the CHANGE SCORE BY message. Here's a simple example using a WHEN THIS SPRITE CLICKED event.

Give it a try. Do you see the value of the SCORE variable going up every time you click?

KEEPING TRACK OF TIME

You may start to notice some "rounded" coding blocks in many of the code categories. These are known as REPORTER blocks, as they report values based on what's happening in your game.

Let's examine one of the REPORTER blocks found in the Sensing menu called the TIMER block. The TIMER block reports the value of time elapsed in seconds since the start flag was clicked.

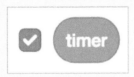

Let's use the TIMER block to stop our game after 10 seconds.

First, we will need the WAIT UNTIL block to pause our code until a TRUE condition occurs. What will be the TRUE/FALSE input on our WAIT UNTIL block? Well, how about if the timer reaches a value greater than 10?

And just for fun, let's have our sprite say "Time's up!" before stopping all of the scripts in our game.

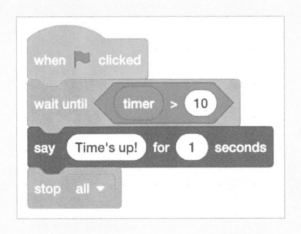

Did you try it? Cool, right?

PICK RANDOM

Another very useful reporter block is PICK RANDOM, located in the Operators menu. This block has a very important function: to create a *random number*.

Why would we need a random number in our game? Here's an example. Let's create an enemy— something scary that will suddenly appear. How about the skeleton? Yes, she's pretty scary! I know I wouldn't want to meet a walking skeleton!

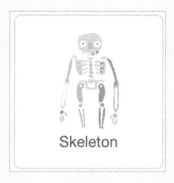

Skeleton

In my imaginary world, skeletons suddenly appear, and you never know when they will show up. So I'm going to show you how to make a sprite suddenly appear, using the HIDE and SHOW blocks.

Between the HIDE and SHOW blocks, we use the WAIT 1 SECOND block to delay the script.

But instead of using the standard 1 second, we'll insert the PICK RANDOM number block inside the WAIT block, as shown in the screenshot.

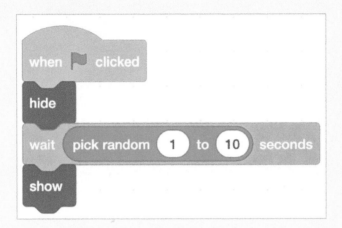

Don't be shy, go ahead and try the code out. But don't be surprised if the skeleton appears when you least expect it. Boo!

X POSITION AND Y POSITION

Knowing where your sprite is on the stage is extremely useful. The reporter blocks known as X POSITION and Y POSITION, found in the Motion block menu, always hold the current position value of the sprite.

So how do you use X POSITION or Y POSITION? Here's an example. Cat says "I've reached the end of the world!" when it moves beyond the edge of the stage. Remember, the farthest x position that is visible on the stage is 240.

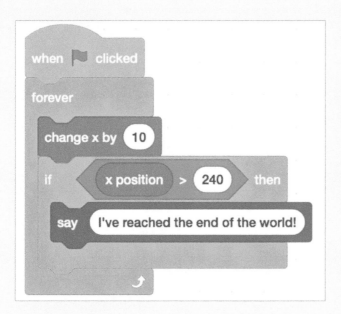

MOUSE X AND MOUSE Y

The MOUSE X and MOUSE Y blocks report the value of the x and y position of the pointer of your computer mouse (or finger touch location). You can find these blocks by clicking on the Sensing menu.

The most common way to use MOUSE X or MOUSE Y blocks is to set the position of a sprite to the same position as your computer mouse pointer's position. Why would you want to do this? Well, it's a fun way to make your sprite follow the mouse pointer. It is also mobile-friendly, because instead of following your mouse, it will follow your finger touch.

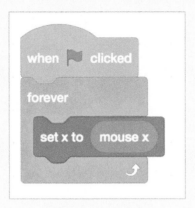

Now, click the green start flag. Then try moving your mouse back and forth across the stage. Does the sprite follow? If so, perfect job! To make the sprite stop following your mouse cursor or finger touch, use the red stop sign (right next to the green flag).

PAINT EDITOR

Hopefully you've explored a bit and discovered that the sprite and backdrop libraries both have wonderful collections of images to use in your games. But that's not all—sometimes you'll need or want to modify them or create your own images.

Whether you start from a blank canvas or modify an existing picture from the library, I'll show you how to use the *paint editor* so you can create unique games.

You can access the paint editor for a sprite by clicking the COSTUMES tab near the top left of the screen.

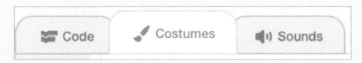

If you have a backdrop already selected, you can modify it with the paint editor by clicking the BACKDROP tab. If you want to create a new backdrop, you can access the paint editor for backdrops by hovering over the BACKDROPS tab in the bottom-right corner, then clicking the paint-brush image.

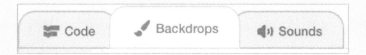

Whether you've opened the paint editor for sprites or backdrops, the toolbars look the same. The best way to learn how to use the different paint editor features is to simply try them out!

Did you check out some of the features? Great! Now, at the bottom of the paint editor, you will see a button that says CONVERT TO BITMAP or CONVERT TO VECTOR. In Scratch 3.0, all sprites start as vector. I want to explain the difference, because it will help you create the best artwork for your games.

MAKE YOUR GAME FUN!

WHAT IS VECTOR?

In vector mode, everything is made with shapes. Every shape can be resized, and you will never lose quality. Even if you draw a line, it is considered a shape. To select a shape, select the pointer from the top of the left menu, and then click on the shape you would like to modify. Maybe you want to change the left arm or right arm—just click them to highlight and they're ready to change.

Here is an example of using the paint bucket in vector mode to change the color of the Scratch cat.

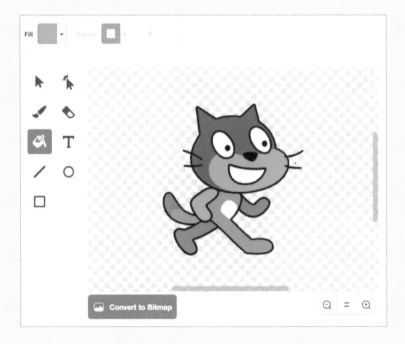

WHAT IS BITMAP?

Everything in bitmap is made of little dots called **pixels**. You can color and draw on the screen just like using crayons on paper. The downside of bitmap is that image quality can get blurry when you increase the size of the sprite. In previous versions of Scratch, the bitmap mode was much easier to use for editing pictures. But in the new version of Scratch 3.0, I find bitmap to be very pixelated and blurry. It all depends on your preference and art style.

CENTER YOUR SPRITE

Always keep the sprite centered on the paint editor. It's a little difficult to see, but in the exact center of the editing screen is a crosshairs symbol. If you don't center your sprite while editing it, you will end up with bugs in your code! Here is a zoomed-in screenshot of the center marker.

Here's an example of a perfectly centered sprite. You can't see the center marker because the sprite is on top of it.

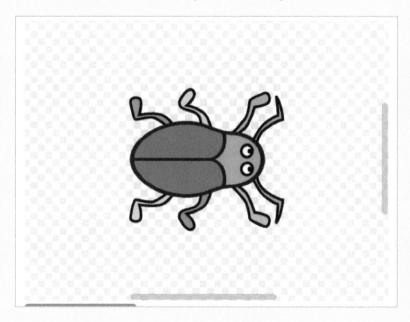

57

DUPLICATING SPRITES

Every sprite you add to your game will have its own script. If you want to duplicate a sprite, you have two options: copy or clone.

COPY

To copy a sprite, simply right-click the sprite (on a computer) or press-and-hold the sprite with your finger (on a tablet), and select "duplicate."

Copying is the best way for beginners to create multiple sprites. Each copy will have exactly the same scripts and perform the exact same actions.

CLONES

If you plan to duplicate a sprite many times, you may want to consider the cloning method. Cloning allows you to duplicate sprites effortlessly, and it keeps your sprite pane from being cluttered with duplicate sprites. Basically, if you are planning to duplicate a sprite more than three times, you should use the cloning method.

Cloning is an advanced method of duplicating a sprite. **Clones** are created by having a sprite create a clone of itself inside its own script. Here's how:

1. Use the CREATE CLONE OF MYSELF Control block to create a clone.

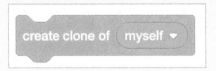

CODING FOR KIDS SCRATCH

2. Click the code. What, nothing happened? But it did! Take your sprite and move it just a tiny bit—look, the clone is under it! Move the original back over the clone for now. We'll move the clone in the next set of directions.

3. Use the WHEN I START AS A CLONE Event block to provide directions for the clones to follow. Clones will only listen to code that starts with this Event block.

Here is a complete example of using the cloning method:

MAKE YOUR GAME FUN!

Look at the clone directions for the code starting with the WHEN I START AS A CLONE block. Notice that I had to move the clone 150 steps away from the original; otherwise, it would have been directly underneath and hidden.

CUSTOM EVENTS USING BROADCAST

Event blocks are used at the beginning of all scripts. The most common Event block, which you've already used several times, is WHEN GREEN FLAG CLICKED.

All scripts that begin with the WHEN GREEN FLAG CLICKED block are meant to be run at the beginning of a game.

But sometimes we don't want scripts to run at the beginning of the game. Sometimes we want to control exactly when a script will run. To do this, we use BROADCAST MESSAGE blocks, which are located in the Event block menu.

The basic technique is to use a BROADCAST block to notify other sprites that an event has occurred. These other sprites will be listening by using the WHEN I RECEIVE Event block.

It might seem a little confusing at first, so let's walk through an example.

BROADCAST MESSAGE

First, let's create a situation where a broadcast would be useful.

Perhaps in our game, we want all of the sprites to hide when the game is over.

This is very easy with a BROADCAST block.

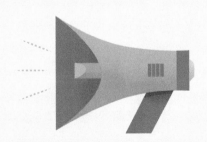

First, let's create the broadcast message by dragging the BROADCAST MESSAGE block to the coding area, and using the drop-down to select "New message."

We can create custom names for our broadcast messages. For my example, I will name it "Game Over."

After the broadcast is named, it will be available in the drop-down menu inside the BROADCAST block.

MAKE YOUR GAME FUN!

Now we need to create a scenario where we would need to broadcast a message in order to hide all of the sprites. For our example, let's say that when the main character (sprite) touches the color red, the game ends.

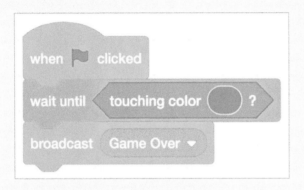

WHEN I RECEIVE MESSAGE

Broadcasting is only half the job! Now we need sprites to be listening for the broadcast. We use the WHEN I RECEIVE MESSAGE Event block to listen for broadcasts.

When a script broadcasts a message, any sprite in the game can listen and react to the broadcast. To make a sprite listen for a broadcast, we use the WHEN I RECEIVE MESSAGE block.

But first, we will need to use the drop-down to make sure we are receiving the "Game Over" message.

Then, we simply build the script we want to run when this event occurs. For my example, I want all sprites to hide themselves. Just don't forget that your sprites will still be hidden when you start the game next time, so be sure to "show" them when the game begins. Here is the complete code to show a sprite when the game begins, but hide it when it receives the message "Game Over."

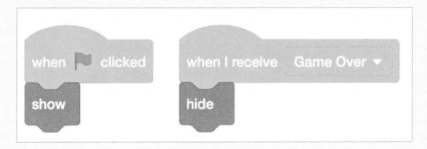

MAKE YOUR GAME FUN!

WHAT JUST HAPPENED? TROUBLESHOOTING TIPS

When you start coding, you're going to face all sorts of surprises. Things may disappear or just not go as planned. Here are some common issues and ways to fix them:

ISSUE	POSSIBLE SOLUTION
Your sprite disappears (you may get a glowing gray box when you try to click in that spot).	When sprites do not show on the stage, and a gray box appears on the stage when you click on their box in the sprite pane, that means they are hidden. You probably clicked the HIDE block at some point. If you click the HIDE block, you must undo it with the SHOW block. Look under the stage for 2 eyeballs that sit side by side. These are the SHOW and HIDE buttons. Click the SHOW one (without the slash). Hopefully this will make it reappear!
You accidentally delete your sprite.	Go to the very top of the page and click on EDIT. Then click RESTORE SPRITE.
You lose your code in the code area.	With version 3.0, it is easy to lose code in the code area. Perhaps you can only see a partial view of the code. The answer to this is to scroll to the left and right in the code area—hopefully it's hiding there and you can move it over into full view!

CODE COMPLETE!

I'm sure everything turned out okay for Mouse. You made him run away next, right? That's how good you're getting! You learned a ton in this chapter, including:

- Knowing to start with a *goal* when you build a video game.

- Selecting a *backdrop* from the Scratch library to make your game look great.

- The Scratch *sound library* has hundreds of sound effects to choose from.

- IF-THEN blocks check if a condition is TRUE. If the condition is TRUE, the code inside the block will run. If the condition is FALSE, the code inside the block will not run.

- *Variables* hold values such as points, lives, or high score.

- Random numbers can make your games more realistic to play (remember how we made the skeleton appear suddenly?) and can be created using the PICK RANDOM block.

- The *paint editor* lets you create your own images or change existing ones.

- You can duplicate sprites in your game by *copying* or *cloning* them.

- You can create your own custom events using BROADCAST MESSAGE blocks.

Great work! You are now officially a Scratch coder. But next is where the fun *really* starts—let's make some games!

PART

2

THE GAMES

Welcome to the games section of *Coding for Kids: Scratch.* **You are probably super excited to start building complete games—I know I am!**

I did my best to keep the games fun but very simple, and I hope you will use your new skills to build them out into more advanced, complete games. Why did I keep them simple? Well, I bet you're very creative and will use these simple games to make really interesting games that are unique to you. I'm also expecting to see your games posted in the Scratch showcase for the world to see. So don't let me down!

I suggest starting with the first game and working through them in order. Of course, you are welcome to skip ahead, but unless you have prior Scratch experience, you might get a little overwhelmed in the later games until you've worked up to them.

Almost all the games work on a computer or a tablet, with the exception of Cat and Mouse Chase, which requires a keyboard to play.

And finally, I created all example games from my experiences as a code instructor. If one of the games looks similar to your idea, I apologize. My goal was to create unique games for this book, but, let's face it, there are millions of kids making Scratch games, and I'm sure there are some Cake Clickers and Scuba Adventure games in the showcase already.

I'm sure you're eager to get going—so turn the page!

CAKE CLICKER

Everyone loves birthdays! Don't you? Cake Clicker is a "clicker" type game, meaning that you will click on the birthday cake to earn points. The goal is to earn points, and when you earn enough, a "Happy Birthday!" message will suddenly appear on the stage.

WHAT YOU'LL LEARN

1. How to increase a variable
2. How to hide and show a sprite

BEFORE YOU BEGIN

1. You'll need to create a variable named "Points." If you need a refresher on how to create a variable, see page 46. Note: When you create variables, you will be offered the option to make the variable "For all sprites" or "For this sprite only." Although it doesn't matter in this game, most of the time you'll want to choose "For all sprites" (until you get into really advanced coding).
2. Choose a backdrop. I chose the backdrop "Party" from the backdrop library. If you need help with backdrops, see page 37.

RECIPE

Cake Clicker is a really easy game to build, and it has a lot of potential for you to make it your own. Don't be afraid to improve my code recipe, as I have seen some amazing clicker games built by first-time coders!

THE CAKE

Cake

You better warm up the oven, because it's time to bake a cake! I'm just kidding; the cake in our game is just a sprite—did you find it yet, inside the sprite library? (See page 13 if you need a quick reminder about the sprite library.)

Here's how to build the script for this game.

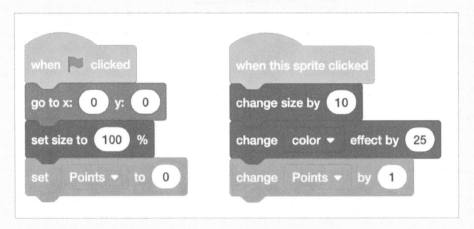

The Cake will require two scripts in its Code Area. The (left-hand) starting script will reset the position, size, and "Points" variable. (See page 69 for more information about variables.) This reset is important, because to make the game fun and exciting, and to show the clicker is working, we will be changing the appearance of the cake. We want the cake to reset to the original look at the start of a new game.

As you can see in the right-hand script, the cake has a WHEN THIS SPRITE CLICKED event. This is the script that will cause the cake to grow in size, change color, and increase the "Points" variable.

"HAPPY BIRTHDAY!" MESSAGE

There are lots of sprites in the library, but there isn't one for "Happy Birthday!" But no need to worry—you will simply paint your own sprite. If you need help painting a sprite, visit page 54.

Hint: To draw a sprite for "Happy Birthday," I used the text-writing tool in the paint editor and font style called "Marker."

Here's what the script for your "Happy Birthday" sprite should look like.

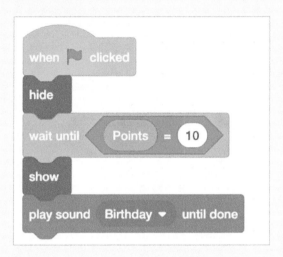

The "Happy Birthday!" message is a surprise, so be sure to hide it at the start of the game, as shown. Remember, wherever the "Happy Birthday!" sprite is on the stage is where it will appear when all the points are reached.

Then use the WAIT UNTIL block to pause the code until "Points" are equal to 10.

Why did I choose the number 10? I just chose it randomly. You can pick a different number if you wish. How about setting it to your age and making it *your* birthday cake?

Lastly, as you can see, I selected the "Birthday" sound from the Sounds menu to play at the end of the script. If you need help adding sounds to your script, visit page 38.

TESTING THE GAME

You worked hard, you coded everything, and now it's time to test out your Cake Clicker!

Go ahead and click the start flag. Did the points reset to zero? Is the cake in the center of the screen? Sounds like you are ready to click! Each time you click the cake, the points should increase by 1. When the points reach 10, the message "Happy Birthday!" should appear on the stage, along with the birthday song.

If everything worked, congratulations! You are a coding rock star on your first try!

But what if it didn't? Never fear, this is a great opportunity to learn about debugging! Just take it one step at a time, and try to figure out what part of the code isn't working properly. Sometimes the smallest errors can cause problems when coding—but solving these problems can be very rewarding.

SET SIZE TO 100%

In Cake Clicker, we increased the size of the cake with every click. If we didn't reset the size to 100% at the start of the game, the cake would never shrink back to its starting size. It would just keep getting bigger until it filled the screen.

NAME YOUR SPRITES

In this example game, the "Game Over" sprite is named the default name: Sprite1. This is okay for a beginner game, but if your games have lots of sprites, this can make it difficult to keep track of sprites. Naming each different sprite eliminates this problem.

WAIT UNTIL IS LIKE A MOUSETRAP

Think of a WAIT UNTIL block as a mousetrap. It waits patiently until the cheese is nibbled, then it springs into action! Unfortunately, like a mousetrap, it can only run a single time.

TRY THESE CODING CHALLENGES

1. Add sounds to each click of the cake.
2. Make a clicker game with a different theme.
3. Make each click worth more points.
4. Make the cake move when you click it.

LATE FOR SCHOOL!

It's time for school, and you overslept! Get out of bed and get dressed as fast as you can! How fast are you? In this game, you will drag-n-drop clothing onto the main character, Harper. But it's a race against the clock, and you only have a limited time before the backdrop switches to the school.

WHAT YOU'LL LEARN

1. Go to a position
2. Use the WAIT block
3. Switch the backdrop

BEFORE YOU BEGIN

You'll need to choose two backdrops for this game. The backdrops I chose are "Bedroom 2" and "School."

RECIPE

Have you ever had the nightmare of arriving at school in only your underpants? How embarrassing! But don't worry, dressing in Scratch is really easy. With a little bit of code and some creative imagination, you'll build your very own Late for School! game and learn to dress in the blink of an eye.

Harper, put some clothes on! You're late for school! And you only have 10 seconds to do it. Wow, you better hurry, because you don't want to arrive at school half-dressed!

HARPER

Harper

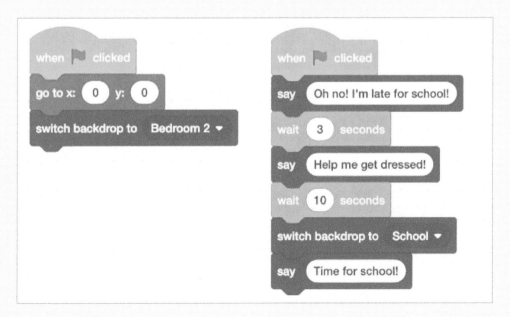

THE GAMES

Let's talk about the two code scripts that Harper will need. The starting script is on the left side. It will position Harper in the center of the stage (x:0, y:0), and it will switch the backdrop to "Bedroom 2."

The right-side script might look confusing, but it's really just a bunch of SAY and WAIT blocks, to make it look like Harper is talking to you. She's saying, "Oh no! I'm late for school!" and then waiting 3 seconds before saying the next phrase.

Just be sure to switch the backdrop at the end of the script to the "School." This might be awkward if she isn't fully dressed yet, but that's the fun of this game—it's not real life!

CLOTHING

Each article of clothing is going to be a unique sprite. If you want four pieces of clothing, then you will need four sprites. I chose the glasses, shirt, shorts, and shoes.

Each clothing sprite will need its own code scripts. But once you code one, you'll know how to code them all.

First, we need to place the clothing sprites exactly where you want them to start. Obviously, you don't want them on Harper—yet!

Now, for each sprite, check the x and y positions by looking in the sprite window. That will be the starting position for the sprite when the green flag is clicked. Each sprite is going to have a different starting position.

For my example, I decided to put the shirt at (x:-143, y:-7) as a random position. You can pick whatever random number you want. Remember, the goal of the game is to move the clothes onto Harper, so they can pop up on the stage wherever.

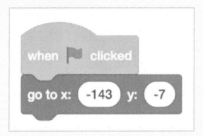

And that's it! The only code necessary for each sprite is the starting position. You will be dragging these clothes to Harper, so you don't need any additional movement code. Remember to pick different random x and y numbers for each piece of clothing so they don't stack on top of each other.

But wait! Scratch doesn't allow you to drag sprites during game play. Well, not unless you set them to "draggable." Make sure each clothing sprite has both the GO TO X Y code block and the SET DRAG MODE block (with "draggable" selected in the pop-up menu).

The great part is, once you figure this out for one sprite, you can repeat the exact same process for all the other clothing sprites. And once you get the hang of positioning sprites, you'll quickly become an expert at it! Now that everything is in place and coded, let's try it out!

TESTING THE GAME

I hope you are more comfortable positioning a sprite on the stage after building this game. It definitely is a challenging skill to learn, but very useful.

If you built this game correctly, when you start the game, Harper will be in her bedroom, with clothing surrounding her. She'll say, "I'm late for school!" and you will drag the clothing onto her before the backdrop switches to the school. Remember, the goal is to get her dressed before time runs out and the backdrop switches, but if you don't, that's okay!

TRY THESE CODING CHALLENGES

1. Customize your game by selecting different costumes.
2. Make a sound each time an article of clothing is clicked.
3. Add more clothing sprites to make the game more challenging.
4. Play a song after the timer is up.

TIPS AND TRICKS

YOU DON'T NEED TO TYPE X AND Y POSITIONS.
HERE'S THE SECRET:

When you drag sprites around the stage using your mouse or finger, the GO TO X Y coding blocks in the code block menu will automatically pre-fill to those x and y positions. The technique is to position your sprites on the stage first, then drag the GO TO block into the code area. If done correctly, you will never need to type a single digit!

GO FORWARD ONE LAYER

Have you ever had a layered birthday cake? Perhaps it had layers of cake, cream, strawberries, and icing. Much like a layered cake, we can have layered sprites! Sprites are placed on top of one another (they overlap), and some may be hidden. You can add the GO FORWARD ONE LAYER block from the Looks menu to your script to fix this problem and show that sprite on top. You can also direct it to go back one layer, or several layers!

DINO HUNT

Dinosaurs disappeared millions of years ago, but guess what? They're back! And it's your job to click on them. With every click, you will hear a pop sound, and a different dinosaur will appear somewhere on the stage. If you find and click on 10 dinosaurs, you win the game!

WHAT YOU'LL LEARN

1. Random position
2. Next costume
3. More about hide and show

BEFORE YOU BEGIN

1. Create a variable named "Points." If you need a refresher on how to create a variable, see page 46.
2. Select a backdrop. I chose the "Jurassic" backdrop from the backdrop library. If you need help with backdrops, see page 37.

RECIPE

Dino Hunt is very easy to code, and it builds upon the techniques that we covered in earlier chapters and used in the Cake Clicker game, including the HIDE and SHOW blocks. These two blocks are really important to master, especially if you want to become a game-building expert!

Let's start with what your costume screen might look like.

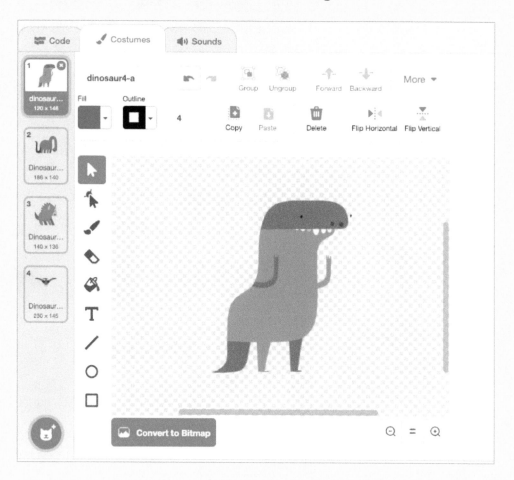

Now listen closely, I'm going to tell you a coding secret. I said that Dino Hunt will have lots of dinosaurs in it, but the truth is, there will only be one dinosaur sprite.

What? I lied? Well, not exactly. Yes, you are only going to add one sprite, but you'll add multiple costumes within that sprite. Each costume will be an entirely different dinosaur!

So, the first step in this process is to look for a dinosaur sprite in the library, and select one you like. After you've selected it, you will need to go into the COSTUMES tab and add multiple dinosaur costumes. To do this, look at the bottom of the left column—you'll see the ADD A COSTUME button (the cat with the + sign). Click this, and scroll down to the dinosaurs. Choose some! As you choose different costumes, you can see them all lined up on the left side of the screen. To see what I mean, look at the previous screenshot of the dinosaur COSTUMES tab (page 81). For more information about costumes, visit page 31.

Okay, now that we have the sprite and costumes ready, the actual scripts are pretty simple. We need two scripts for the dinosaur sprite. The first script is the starting script, and the second is the WHEN THIS SPRITE CLICKED script, which makes the action happen.

This is what your code will look like.

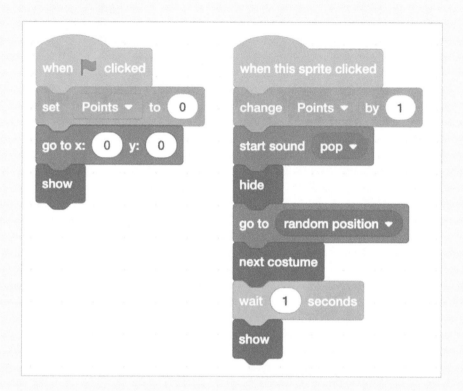

The starting script resets the points, positions the sprite in the center (x:0, y:0), and sets the visibility to show. Why do we need to show the sprite? Well, because it might be hidden from previous play, so we want it visible when we start each game.

The second script starts with a WHEN THIS SPRITE CLICKED Event block. The code blocks are then run in order, from top to bottom, so it's pretty easy to figure out what it does. The order of the code is extremely important in a script, but you can always experiment with your own ideas.

So, what exactly happens to the dinosaur after it is clicked? Well, first the points increase by 1, then a "pop" sound plays. Next, the sprite is hidden and moved to a random location. Then the costume is changed, and it waits for 1 second before showing itself.

Go ahead and try it. Did it work? If so, good job! That was a lot of code. If not, double-check your code.

Now let's add some sound and a pop-up message that says, "You Win!"

Here's what the code will look like.

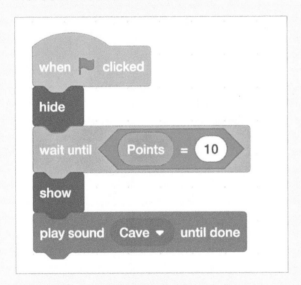

There are lots of sprites in the library, but there isn't one for "You Win!" That means you'll need to paint your own sprite with the words "You Win!" If you need help painting your own sprites, go back to the Paint Editor section on page 54.

The "You Win!" message should only show at the end of the game, so be sure to hide it at the beginning of the code block, as shown.

Then, you'll use the WAIT UNTIL block to pause the code until "Points" are equal to 10.

Why did I choose the number 10? Oh no, that's the same number I used in the Cake Clicker game. Perhaps I really like the number 10? You can make your own rules and use any number you like.

Lastly, I selected the "Cave" sound from the Sounds menu to play at the end of the script. "Cave" is a fun melody, but you are free to make your own sound selection. If you need help adding sounds to your script, visit page 38.

TESTING THE GAME

If you coded Dino Hunt correctly, the game should start with a dinosaur in the center of the stage. When you click it, it should disappear, and a different dinosaur should appear in a random location. After you click 10 dinosaurs, the "You Win!" message should appear.

TIPS AND TRICKS

SPRITES VS. BACKDROPS

New Scratch coders often confuse sprites and backdrops. Just remember, you can only have one backdrop showing at a time, but you can have multiple sprites showing at the same time.

CODE RUNS LIKE A WATERFALL

Code is not made of water. But the computer reads the code from top to bottom, similar to a waterfall. If your code isn't working correctly, start at the top and work your way down, looking for errors.

TRY THESE CODING CHALLENGES

1. Change the size of the dinosaurs.
2. Change the sounds.
3. Animate each dinosaur when it appears.

CAT AND MOUSE CHASE

Scratch cat is on a mission to catch mice for dinner. To win, help Scratch cat find five mice. But don't touch the dog or it's game over!

WHAT YOU'LL LEARN

1. Key arrow-pressed
2. Change x and change y

BEFORE YOU BEGIN

1. Create a variable named "Mice caught." If you need a reminder on how to create a variable, see page 46.
2. Select a backdrop. I chose the "Bedroom 1" backdrop from the backdrop library. If you need help with backdrops, see page 37.

RECIPE

Cat and Mouse Chase is an old-school Scratch game, and it introduces many of the skills needed for advanced game-building. **Note:** This game requires a keyboard to play and may not work well on a tablet.

CAT

As I'm guessing you know, the cat sprite can be found in the sprite library, and it comes standard with every new blank project. I changed the name using the sprite window to "Cat," as it was called "Sprite1" origi-nally. (I did this by typing in the space next to the label "Sprite" at the top of the pane.) I like the name "Cat" a lot more, don't you?

Cat

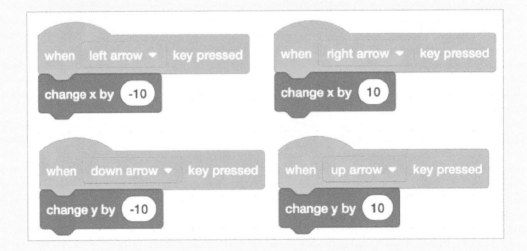

In this game, the cat will move around the stage looking for mice. The cat will move by changing its x position and y position. The code on the previous page shows the easiest way to code this technique.

The good part about this movement script is that it's fairly quick and easy to build. The bad part is that the movement of the cat will be very clunky and jerky. Try it for yourself. You can see that the cat "jumps" around and the movement isn't very professional.

Here is the professional way to code movement that happens when certain keys are pressed.

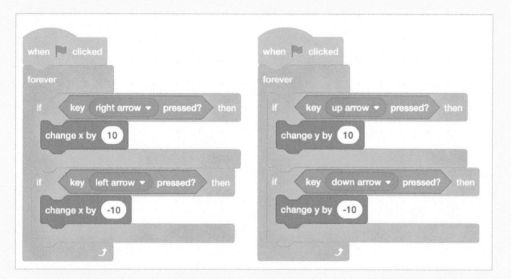

Why are these scripts better than the previous ones? The secret is in how the Scratch editor and your computer are interpreting the code. Sometimes putting code in a different order or using different types of blocks can achieve a similar result, but with differences in performance. In this case, the movement became smoother, but it required more coding blocks to create the script. Is it worth the extra effort? Only you can decide!

THE GAMES

Don't believe me? Try it yourself. Copy the code. Then click the start flag, and you will actually see these scripts glowing yellow. Remember that this means the computer is running the code.

MOUSE

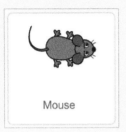

Mouse

The mouse sprite is found in the sprite library. It was actually named "Mouse1," but I changed the name in the sprite window to just "Mouse."

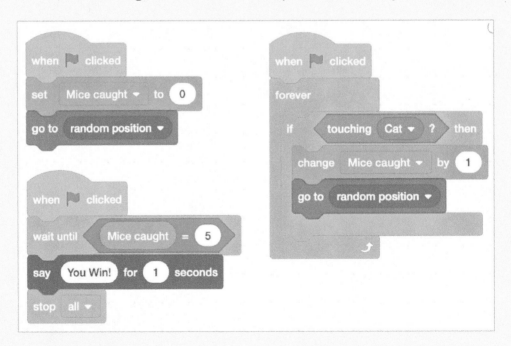

As you can see in the screenshot, you'll need three scripts for the mouse to work correctly.

The first script, (the top-left one), is the starting code. It sets the variable "Mice caught" to 0 and moves the mouse to a random location.

The right-side script is a conditional IF-THEN block that is checking to see when the mouse is touching the cat. If the condition is TRUE, then the "Mice caught" variable will increase by 1 and the mouse will move to a random position on the stage.

The bottom-left script is a WAIT UNTIL block that will run when the "Mice caught" variable equals 5. You can also increase this value to make the game more challenging. After this script runs, the STOP ALL block ends the game.

DOG

The dog sprite is also located in—yes, you guessed it—the sprite library. The dog's role in the game is to glide around the stage, possibly touching the cat and ending the game.

Dog2

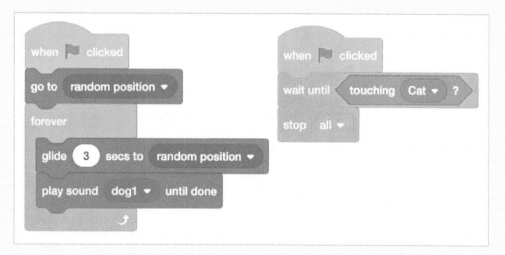

THE GAMES

The left-side script is the starting code for the dog. First, clicking the flag will move the dog to a random position. Then, we create a FOREVER loop that contains two actions: glide to a random position and play a sound.

The right-side script is a WAIT UNTIL block that is patiently waiting for the dog to touch the cat. If this event occurs, then the game will end with the STOP ALL block.

TIPS AND TRICKS

SAY OR THINK? WHAT'S THE DIFFERENCE?

SAY and THINK code blocks do the same thing. It really just depends on whether you want the sprite to appear to be saying the words or thinking them. It's up to you!

STOP ALL

In Cat and Mouse Chase, we use the STOP ALL block to end the game. Just remember this: STOP ALL only stops scripts that begin with WHEN GREEN FLAG CLICKED. In the Cake Clicker and Dino Hunt games, STOP ALL would not have stopped game play, because those games used WHEN THIS SPRITE CLICKED.

TRY THESE CODING CHALLENGES

1. Add more dogs or mice.
2. Make the cat point in the direction that it is moving.
3. Make the dog move at random speeds.
4. Add a "Game Over" sprite or backdrop.

SCUBA ADVENTURE

Does swimming with sharks sound exciting? Then you'll love Scuba Adventure! In this thrilling underwater adventure game, you are a scuba diver searching the ocean for fish, while avoiding the ferocious shark! Find enough fish and you win the game. But, if you touch the shark, he will eat all of your fish and you will have to start over.

WHAT YOU'LL LEARN

1. Move towards the mouse pointer
2. If touching
3. Glide to random position
4. Reset points

93

BEFORE YOU BEGIN

1. Create a variable named "Fish found." If you need a refresher on how to create a variable, see page 46.
2. Select a backdrop. I chose the "Underwater 1" backdrop from the backdrop library. For help with backdrops, see page 37.

RECIPE

I love scuba diving. I love the magical beauty of swimming with tropical fish. But let's be clear on one thing: Collecting fish from the wild is wrong! Thankfully, this is just a game, and no fish were harmed in the making of this game.

Scuba Adventure is a follow-the-mouse-pointer style game (objects move to follow your mouse pointer). It works well on computers, laptops, tablets, and mobile devices. Even cavemen millions of years ago would enjoy this style of game control. What? Cavemen? Really?

DIVER

To start, you'll need to select a main character—whoops, I meant to say sprite. Obviously, this is an underwater scuba game, so I chose an appropriate diver sprite from the Scratch library.

The code for the diver is much simpler than the code for the fish or the shark. Why? Because the diver simply follows the mouse pointer around the screen.

The left-side code is our starting script. It resets any changes from the last game and makes sure the sprite is the correct size. I felt the diver sprite was a little large, so I set the size to 70%.

Diver2

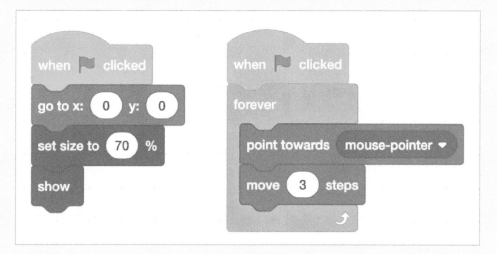

The right-side coding script is the movement code. This type of movement is known as "follow the mouse pointer." If coded correctly, the diver should follow your mouse around the stage. The FOREVER loop keeps the diver moving and the MOVE 3 STEPS block specifies how far the diver moves. If you are coding or playing the game on a tablet, the diver should follow your finger touch.

There is a known bug that if the diver touches the mouse-pointer, he will start flipping left-right in a frenzy. If you want to eliminate this bug, here is what to do: Insert an IF-THEN-ELSE block inside of the diver movement code's FOREVER loop. Then insert the condition, "touching mouse-pointer" then move 0 steps. In the "Else" area of the block, insert the actual movement code. It's a little bit advanced, but I bet you'll figure it out!

FISH

The fish sprite in the Scratch library is really useful because it comes with lots of costumes already installed. Similar to the Dino Hunt game, you will only need to code a single fish, and it will simply use a NEXT COSTUME block to change its appearance.

Fish

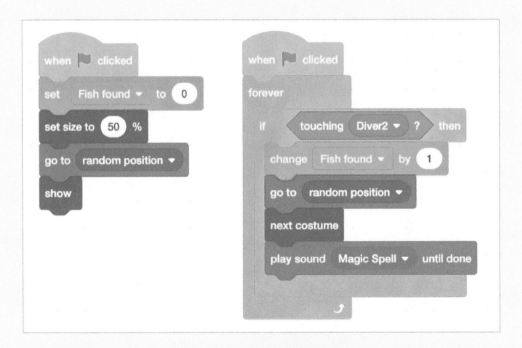

In our game, the diver will be collecting fish. Rather than naming this variable "Points," I will name it "Fish found."

The fish code has two main scripts. The first (left-side) script is the starting script, and it resets anything that may have occurred in previous game play. Just like the Cake Clicker game, we need to reset the sprite so it is ready for a new game.

The second (right-side) script is designed to forever be checking if the fish is touching the diver. Why forever? Because we want to constantly be checking if the fish is touching the diver. If they touch, we have a long list of code that will then run, including changing the variable, moving to a random position, switching costumes, and playing a sound.

If the fish is touching the diver, that means the diver caught it—so it updates the "Fish found" points! Then, we need the fish to move to a random position and change costume so it looks like a new fish. The sound plays and lets us know we have successfully caught a fish!

SHARK

There are a couple of options for sharks in the Scratch library, and I chose the sprite listed as "Shark" because it is very realistic looking. Unfortunately, this shark doesn't have a great selection of costumes in its Costume menu. If you are very brave, you could always draw another costume, or even draw your own shark sprite!

Shark

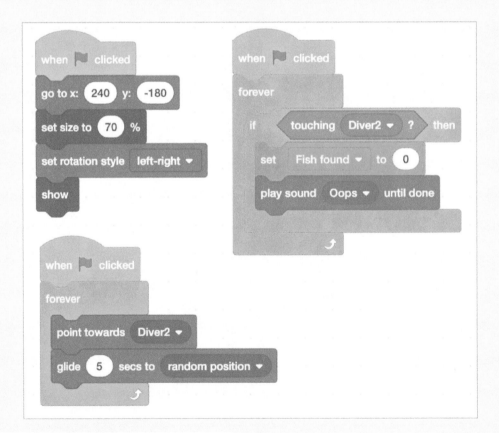

In our game, sharks don't eat divers (whew!)—they just steal our fish! And let's have our shark move around the stage randomly. This will make it easier for us to stay away from the shark.

The shark code has three unique (and somewhat long) scripts.

The first script (top-left) is the starting script. Just like the diver, I made the shark a little bit smaller by setting the size to 70%. I also made sure the shark starts in the bottom corner of the screen (x:240, y:-180). This will give you enough time to avoid him when the game starts.

You may notice I set the rotation style to left-right. Why do we set the rotation style? Well, if you don't, the shark will flip upside down when it turns to the left (see page 27).

The second script (bottom-left) is the movement script. This script controls—you got it—the movement of the shark. Basically, the movement of the shark is inside a FOREVER loop, constantly gliding towards a random position. I made the glide speed 5 seconds, but you can change this number depending on how fast you want the shark to swim and how hard you want the game to be.

I'm sure you are also wondering why I pointed the shark toward the diver, considering that it doesn't actually change the direction he is moving. I did this to hide a bug in my code. Which bug? Well, if you don't put in that code, the shark will often swim backward. Have you ever seen a shark swim backward? I haven't. Pointing the shark towards the diver is not a perfect fix, but it works.

Finally, the third script (top-right) is the "if touching" script. You should immediately notice that when the shark touches the diver, it sets the variable to 0, rather than reducing it by 1. Why are we setting it to 0?

Well, in my opinion, the shark would be super greedy and eat all of the fish, no matter how many I have. By setting the "Fish found" to 0, we are basically restarting the game. I think it's a fun way to play, but you are welcome to be creative with your own ideas.

YOU WIN!

Yes, once again, you will need to paint your own sprite with the words "You Win!" If you need help with the paint editor, visit page 54.

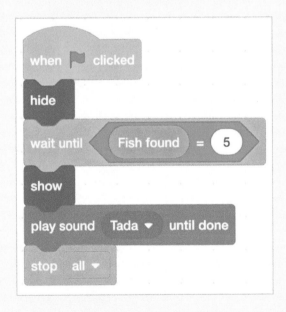

CODING FOR KIDS SCRATCH

The "You Win!" message should only show at the end of the game, so be sure to hide it at the beginning of the code block as shown.

Then, you'll use the WAIT UNTIL block to pause the code until the number of "Fish found" is equal to 5.

I choose the number 5 because I thought it was a nice amount of fish to find, but you can pick any number you want!

Lastly, I selected the "Tada" sound from the Sounds menu to play at the end of the script. Go ahead—select your own sounds for this fun adventure game.

TESTING THE GAME

If you coded Scuba Adventure correctly, the diver should follow the mouse pointer around the screen and the "Fish found" variable should increase whenever the diver touches a fish. The fish sprite should move to a random position and change costumes after each touch, so it looks like a new fish. The shark should glide around randomly to different locations on the stage.

If the diver touches the shark, the "Fish found" variable resets to 0. If five fish are found, the "You Win!" sprite appears on the stage, and the game stops.

TRY THESE CODING CHALLENGES

1. Add underwater sounds.
2. Add additional types of fish (octopus, jellyfish, etc.).
3. Add more sharks.
4. Make some fish more valuable than other fish.

SPACE JUMPER

In a galaxy far away, there lives a space alien named Pico. Pico's main purpose in life is to jump over beach balls, which are always rolling in his direction. As silly as it sounds, if he ever touches a beach ball, he will lose a life. Fortunately, Pico has three lives!

WHAT YOU'LL LEARN

1. Repeat blocks
2. Creating a "Lives" variable
3. Animation

BEFORE YOU BEGIN

1. Create a variable named "Lives." If you need a refresher on how to create a variable, see page 46.
2. Select a backdrop. I chose the "Space City 1" backdrop from the backdrop library. If you need help with backdrops, see page 37.
3. Add sprites from the library for Pico Walking and Beachball prior to coding this game. We need to add them prior to coding because, if we don't, then the sprite names will not appear in the drop-down selectors for our IF touching blocks.

RECIPE

Space Jumper uses the REPEAT block to create very smooth jumping motions. One of my pet peeves for beginner Scratch games is the choppy animation of poorly coded movement. C'mon, we can do better! In fact, I hope you use Space Jumper as the beginning of a very elaborate, complex game. I can't wait to see what you will build!

PICO

First, you must find the "Pico Walking" sprite in the library. This is a great sprite for this game, because there are multiple costumes included, which, when put together, create a walking animation.

Pico will start with three lives. Everyone in the universe knows that Picos are born with three lives. Okay, I made that up, but let's just pretend it's true!

Pico Walking

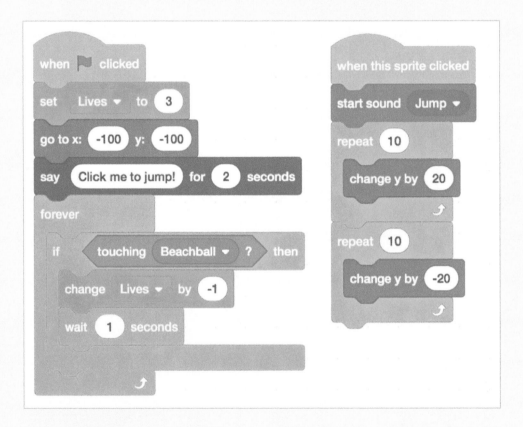

There are two coding scripts for Pico: the starting script (left-side) and the jumping script (right-side).

In the starting script, we want to set the "Lives" variable to 3, and we'll position Pico at the bottom-left of the stage (x:-100, y:-100). We will have Pico say, "Click me to jump," so the player understands how the game play works.

To keep things simple, I have included the "if touching Ball" script inside of the starting script block. The basic idea is that whenever Pico touches the ball, he will lose one life.

Why is there a WAIT 1 SECOND block after Pico loses one life? That is actually to fix a bug in this code. The 1 second gives enough time for the ball to finish rolling past Pico without him losing more than one life.

Now let's focus on the right-side script, which gives Pico the ability to jump. I chose to use a WHEN THIS SPRITE CLICKED block to trigger this event, but you can use a different keyboard event, such as WHEN SPACE PRESSED. Just remember that whatever Pico says has to match the code. So, if you chose WHEN SPACE PRESSED, make Pico say "Press space bar to jump!" instead.

There are many ways to "jump" a sprite, but my personal favorite is to use a REPEAT block to make the jump movement look very smooth and professional.

Let's explain the jumping script.

The first REPEAT block moves Pico up, and the second REPEAT block moves Pico down. We don't actually need to use the REPEAT blocks to create an up-down action, but I find the REPEAT blocks naturally create a very smooth up-down movement. Be sure to fiddle with the REPEAT block values to create your own crazy jumping style. And perhaps you might even find a better way to jump Pico!

BEACH BALL

Beachball

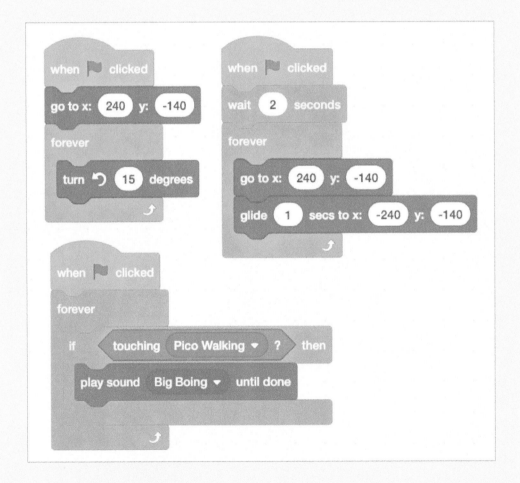

Perhaps a game where beach balls roll around on a planet in outer space is somewhat absurd. But that's the beauty of Scratch—your imagination can run wild!

Let's break down the code for the beach ball.

The beach ball will continually roll from the right to the left side of the screen. To begin the game, we should make sure the ball is positioned in the correct location on the stage: (x:240, y:-140). To create a rolling animation, you simply need TURN 15 DEGREES inside a FOREVER loop.

Now that the beach ball is rolling, let's move it across the screen. To do this, we use the GLIDE block. Because we want to repeat the movement over and over, we wrap the movement code inside a FOREVER loop. We can control the speed of the movement by changing the number of seconds the glide movement takes. I found that 1 second is a great speed for the ball to move across the stage, but this is a number that can be adjusted depending on your skill level. Then, once the ball touches Pico, it will play the "Big Boing" sound.

GAME OVER

Yes, you will need to paint your own sprite with the words "Game Over!" If you need help with the paint editor, visit page 54.

The "Game Over!" message should only show at the end of the game, so be sure to hide it at the beginning of the code block, as shown in the screenshot.

Then, use the WAIT UNTIL block to pause the code until "Lives" equals 0.

TESTING THE GAME

If you coded Space Jumper correctly, Pico should jump when you click him directly (or if you press the space bar, if you used the WHEN SPACE PRESSED block). Pico should have three lives when the game begins, and he should lose a life every time he touches the ball.

CODING FOR KIDS SCRATCH

TIPS AND TRICKS

WHAT GOES UP MUST COME DOWN

Scratch doesn't have gravity. If your Pico jumps in the air and doesn't come down, then you probably forgot to change the y value to a negative number (example: -20).

ENDLESS RUNNER GAMES

Space Jumper is very similar to endless runner games like Jet Pack Joyride or Geometry Dash. Creating a moving background in Scratch is very complex, but making other objects (clouds, birds, and trees) fly past can give the sense of movement.

TRY THESE CODING CHALLENGES

1. Earn points for jumping over the ball.
2. Create a "You Win!" sprite.
3. Add more sounds to the game.
4. Make the ball and Pico disappear at the end of the game.

BALLOON POP!

The sky is falling! Run for your lives! Wait, those are balloons falling. Don't crabs love to pop balloons? Perhaps not, but in our game, our fearless crab will attempt to pop every balloon before it touches the ground.

WHAT YOU'LL LEARN

1. Set x position
2. Repeat until
3. Broadcasting messages

BEFORE YOU BEGIN

1. Create a variable named "Balloons popped." If you need a refresher on how to create a variable, see page 46.
2. Select a backdrop. I chose the "Blue Sky" backdrop from the backdrop library. If you need help with backdrops, see page 37.
3. Add sprites from the sprite library for this game, including "Crab" and "Balloon1." You'll need the sprites to be added to the sprite pane prior to coding the game, or you will not have access to those sprite names in the drop-down selectors.
4. Add the sound "Squish Pop" from the sound library (see page 38).

RECIPE

Crabs catching balloons? Has the world gone mad? This game is a bit goofy. But the coding techniques are universal and can be applied to endless game ideas. My advice is to build the basic game, then go wild making it your own unique creation. Good luck!

CRAB

Crab

Find the "Crab" sprite in the library. Fortunately, it comes with two costumes—these let you animate the claws.

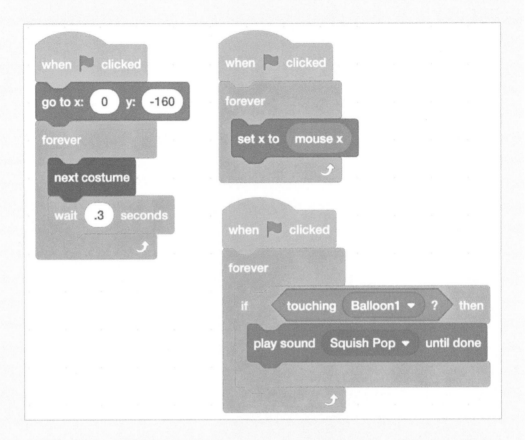

Crabs naturally move left-right, and they have wonderful claws for catching balloons. Did I say catching? I meant popping!

The crab sprite will start the game at the bottom-center of the screen (x:0, y:160) in your first block of code.

Remember how the crab's costumes let you animate the claws? Simply put NEXT COSTUME inside a FOREVER loop and you will see the animation. I slowed it down with a WAIT 0.3 SECONDS block.

CODING FOR KIDS SCRATCH

Since the crab will move left-right, we will be only changing the x position (left-right) and not the y position (up-down).

An interesting way to move a sprite left-right is to set the x position of the sprite to the x position of the mouse pointer. This might seem confusing at first, but once you try it, I'm sure it will make more sense.

First, you will need to locate the MOUSE X code block from the Sensing block menu. The MOUSE X block always contains the value of your mouse pointer's x position on the screen. In other words, if your mouse pointer is at (x:160), then the MOUSE X block will have the value of 160.

Are you wondering why I wrapped the SET X block inside a FOREVER loop? The FOREVER loop will cause the crab to constantly move when your mouse moves. Try it—I think you'll like it! Then, when the crab touches the balloon, the game will play the "Squish Pop" sound.

BALLOON

Balloon1

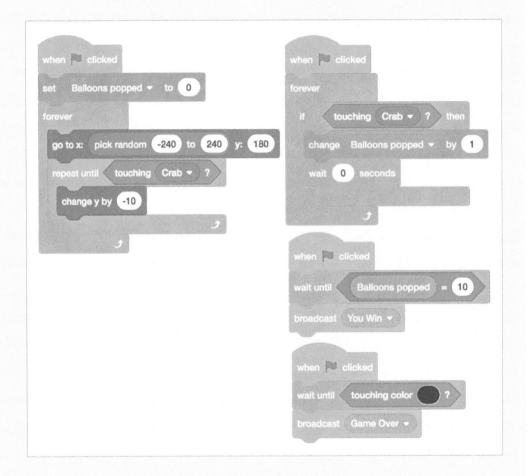

Are you ready to make balloons fall from the sky? Okay, this is not normal, considering that balloons don't usually fall. But I had to make a choice: either the crab flies, or the balloons fall. I decided to go with balloons falling.

There are four separate scripts in our balloon code, and I combined the starting script with the movement code in the first script block (top-left). In the starting code block, we'll set the "Balloons popped" variable to a value of 0. In the same starting block, we'll also add the movement.

The balloon is going to start at the top of the screen (y:180) and fall to the bottom of the stage. The x position will be chosen by the PICK RANDOM block—this will make the balloons drop from different locations in the sky. Then, to make a sprite fall, you simply change the y position by -10 inside of a REPEAT loop. Using the REPEAT UNTIL TOUCHING CRAB block will provide an end to the REPEAT loop—otherwise, the balloon would fall forever.

Test the code and see if it makes the balloon fall from the sky to the ground.

If it works, then let's add some more complexity to this code.

In this game, there will be both "Game Over!" and "You Win!" sprites.

Let's build two different WAIT UNTIL code scripts, one for each ending.

The basic idea is that points are earned when the crab pops balloons, but the game immediately ends if a balloon touches the ground. Since we will have two ending scenarios—win and lose—it is best to use the BROADCAST MESSAGE block to trigger the end of the game.

The first script will check if the "Balloons popped" variable equals 10, and if so, the game will broadcast the "You Win!" message.

The second script will sense if the balloon touches the ground (color: brown), and if so, it will broadcast the message "Game Over!"

If you need a review on broadcast messages, see page 60.

GAME OVER

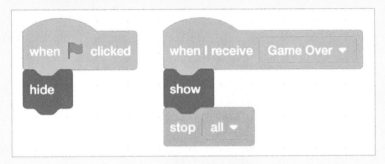

You will need to create a "Game Over!" sprite yourself.

The "Game Over!" sprite will be hidden at the start of the game. When the message "Game Over!" is received, it will show itself and stop all scripts.

If you need a review on creating sprites yourself, see page 54. To review the lesson on receiving messages, see page 62.

YOU WIN

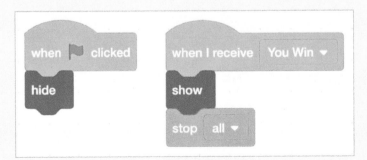

You'll also need to create a "You Win!" sprite. Like the "Game Over!" sprite, the "You Win!" sprite will be hidden at the start of the game. When the message "You Win!" is received, it will show itself and stop all scripts.

TESTING THE GAME

If coded correctly, the crab should move left and right following the position of the mouse pointer (or finger touch). Random balloons should fall from the sky and continue falling until they touch either the crab or the ground. If the crab "pops" 10 balloons, the "You Win!" message appears. If a balloon touches the ground, the "Game Over!" message appears.

TIPS AND TRICKS

SET X VS. CHANGE X BLOCKS

Be careful not to confuse SET X with CHANGE X. We need the crab's position to be exactly the same as the mouse pointer (so you can control it), so we must be careful to use the SET X and not CHANGE X.

IF TOUCHING COLOR

If you use IF TOUCHING COLOR Sensing blocks, be careful that the color doesn't exist somewhere else in your game. In this game, I used the "Blue Sky" backdrop, so the color brown only occurs on the ground, making it safe to use.

TRY THESE CODING CHALLENGES

1. Add background music.
2. Make the crab have three lives before the game ends.
3. Change the costume of the balloon to different objects or animals.

CRYSTAL KEEPER

Dragons and crystals and castles—oh my! This game will have you buried in sparkling crystals . . . or facing off against a fire-breathing dragon! With a little practice, though, you'll master being a crystal keeper in no time!

WHAT YOU'LL LEARN

1. Ask blocks
2. Answer blocks
3. Cloning
4. If-else blocks

119

BEFORE YOU BEGIN

Select a backdrop. I chose the "Castle 1" backdrop from the backdrop library. If you need help with backdrops, see page 37.

RECIPE

I love treasures and secret passwords. If you do, too, then you'll love Crystal Keeper. My example game is very simple, but it teaches the basics of asking for user input and touches on the power of cloning. Have fun building, modifying, and designing your own secret password games!

NANO

Nano

In our game, Nano is the gatekeeper to a treasure of beautiful crystals. There are lots of fun sprites that would do an equally good job, but Nano is just too cute for me to resist. Perhaps you'll choose a monster? Or a unicorn?

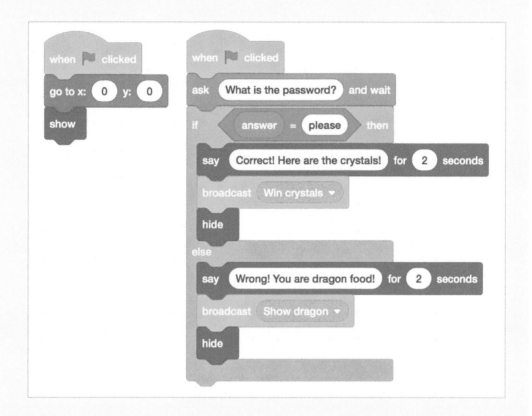

The starting code for Nano is very basic: Put her in the center (x:0, y:0) and set the visibility to show using a SHOW block.

The second code script contains the ASK block. The ASK block is the only block that captures input from the user. Basically, the video game will ask you a question. It will do this by showing a text box at the bottom of the screen.

After you fill in the answer to the question, the computer will hold your response inside a premade variable called ANSWER. (Note: The ANSWER block is found in the Sensing menu. It always contains the value of the response to the ASK block, meaning you will have to type in the answer text so the computer knows when the answer is correct. They are a team and should be used together.)

For our game, the question will be, "What is the password?" There will be two possible outcomes for the question: either you answered correctly, or you didn't. Whenever you have two possible outcomes, you should use an IF-ELSE block. An IF-ELSE block is similar to the IF-THEN block because a condition must be met for something to happen. With an IF-THEN block, *if* the condition is met, *then* something happens.

But an IF-ELSE block adds another step. *If* the condition is met, *then* something happens. *If* it is not met, something *else* happens.

DRAGON

Dragon

Dragons breathe fire and are extremely dangerous. Be *very* careful when you code the dragon sprite. Just kidding! But this will make a great sprite to scare away anyone without the correct password.

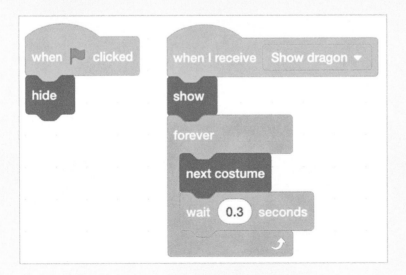

There is a wonderful dragon sprite in the library that has multiple costumes and is very easy to animate with the NEXT COSTUME block.

The code for the dragon is very simple. The dragon is hidden at the start of the game, waiting for the message "Show dragon" to be broadcasted from the Nano sprite. After receiving the "Show dragon" message, the dragon will show itself and forever switch costumes to create an epic fire-breathing animation.

CRYSTAL

Crystal

Are you ready to make priceless crystals suddenly cover the stage? How many crystals do you desire? 100? 200? Okay, how about 300 crystals? Let's make it happen! Find the crystal sprite in the library.

We use cloning when we want to duplicate a single sprite without creating additional sprites. Can you imagine creating 300 sprites? It would take forever. But with cloning, it's as easy as pie.

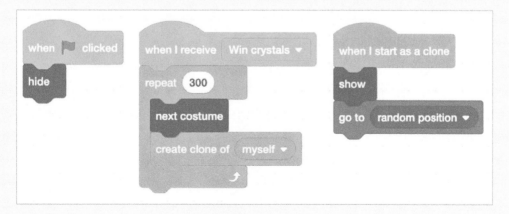

For our crystal code, we first hide the sprite in the starting script. Then we wait for the message, "Win crystals." This begins the REPEAT block that creates clones. And just for fun, I added the NEXT COSTUME block so that each clone has a different costume.

Clones always need their own WHEN I START AS A CLONE Event blocks. They don't listen to start flags or any other Event blocks. For our game, we simply want the clones to show themselves and appear at random locations. If done correctly, the 300 crystal clones should fill the screen. It should be beautiful and sort of overwhelming at the same time!

TESTING THE GAME

When you play Crystal Keeper, you will immediately be asked by Nano to enter the password. If you enter the wrong password, you will see a fire-breathing dragon appear on the stage. If you enter the correct password, the screen will suddenly be filled with hundreds of crystals.

TRY THESE CODING CHALLENGES

1. Try adding additional questions to Nano's script.
2. Add sound effects and music.
3. Make Nano move across the screen when the game starts.

TIPS AND TRICKS

CLONING

Cloning is a great way to duplicate a sprite. But be careful not to make too many clones in one game; that will keep the game from running smoothly. How many is too many? I guess you'll just need to experiment and find out for yourself!

BACKPACK

Are you curious what that BACKPACK tab is at the bottom of the Scratch page? This is actually a storage area that you can use for saving scripts to be accessed in other games. To save scripts inside the **backpack**, simply drag the block in and release. How cool is that?

BEETLE ROAD

Chances are, you've played a game like this in the arcade. It's a favorite—and now you can make it! In Beetle Road, the objective is to help the beetle jump across the busy freeway. Yes, it's dangerous, but our jumping beetle is under your fearless control. How many levels can you pass before your beetle gets squished?

WHAT YOU'LL LEARN

1. "Start"/"Game Over" backdrops
2. More on cloning

BEFORE YOU BEGIN

1. Create a variable named "Points." If you need a refresher on how to create a variable, see page 46.
2. Create several backdrops (see the screenshots on page 37). Beetle Road uses custom-made backdrops, which are described in these instructions.

RECIPE

Beetle Road is a mobile-friendly game, meaning that it should work well on tablets as well as computers. It is obviously inspired by classics like Frogger and Crossy Road, which are two of my favorites. It's always fun to be inspired by other people's games—just make sure that you add your own unique twist, and do your best not to simply copy other Scratchers' games from the showcase.

BACKDROPS

Let's take a quick look at the three backdrops you will need to draw in order for this game to work properly. Remember, only one backdrop can be seen on the stage at a time, so the additional backdrops will need to be added inside the BACKDROPS tab, similar to adding costumes on a sprite.

Read on to see some examples and close-ups of each backdrop that I drew for this game.

Quick tip: When painting backdrops, the paint bucket will not fill the entire canvas with color unless you have first drawn a shape. I used only the Rectangle-Tool and Text-Tool to paint everything in my backdrops. It takes some practice, but I know you will quickly learn how to paint amazing backdrops!

The "Start" Backdrop

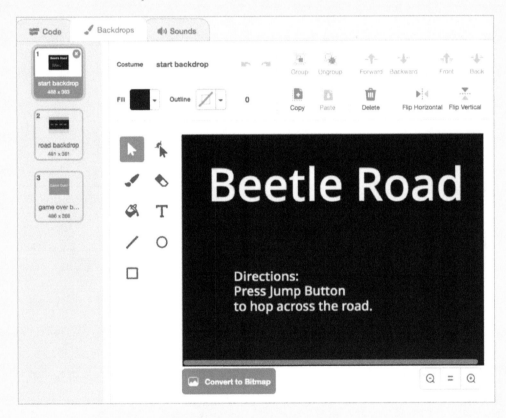

The "Road" Backdrop

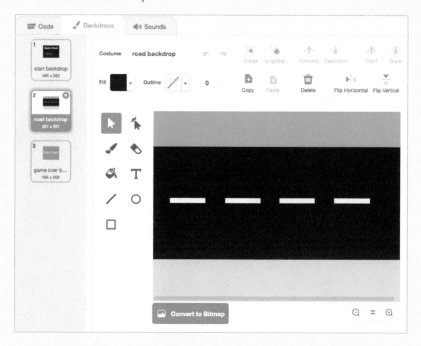

The "Game Over" Backdrop

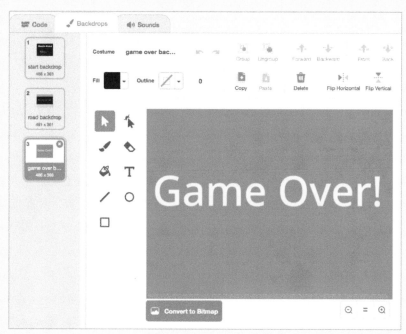

BACKDROP CODE

Beetle Road uses backdrops to create three distinct scenes: the "Start" backdrop, the "Road" backdrop, and the "Game Over" backdrop.

Unlike the backdrops in our other example games, the backdrops in this game require their own codes in the code area.

The backdrop scripts will determine which backdrop is showing, depending on the messages they receive.

At the start of the game, we want to show the "Start" backdrop. Then, when we receive the message "Start Game," we will want the backdrop to switch to the "Road" backdrop.

And finally, when the "Game Over" message is received, the backdrop will switch to the "Game Over" backdrop, and the STOP ALL block will end the game.

I realize that this code might be a little confusing, considering that you haven't yet coded the sprites that broadcast these messages! But these kinds of challenges help you become a better coder. Just try your best, and I'm sure you will do great!

START BUTTON

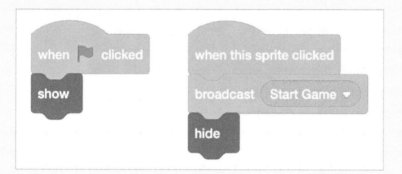

A start button is a professional way to begin a game. I created the button by choosing "Button2" in the sprite library, and then I added the text "Start" using the paint editor.

As you can see in the screenshots, the code for the start button is very simple. You want it to show itself at the start of the game and broadcast the message "Start Game" when it's clicked. It's a simple script, but very effective. And remember, the backdrop is waiting for that message "Start Game," so you are well on your way to building a complete Beetle Road game!

JUMP BUTTON

Jump, beetle, jump!

This jump button sprite was made the same way as the start button. I decided to add the JUMP button to the game in order for the game to truly be mobile-friendly.

The first step to coding the JUMP button is to decide when it will appear on the stage. I want it to be hidden on the start screen but show up when the game begins. And finally, I want it to disappear when the "Game Over" message is received.

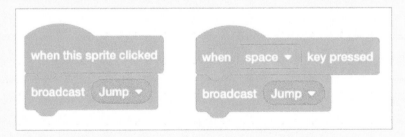

Now, let's create the functionality of the JUMP button. Its job is to tell the beetle to jump by broadcasting the "Jump" message. I decided to give you two options in the game for jumping. Can you guess what the two ways are? Yes, you can click the JUMP button, or you can press the space bar. You are welcome to add more ways to jump, as well.

BEETLE

The beetle is our main character in the game. The beetle will start at the bottom of the stage and then jump across the road until it reaches the other side. When it reaches the other side, it will be transported to the start again, where it will repeat the dangerous trek across the street.

To start, we will need to hide the beetle sprite. Why would we hide it? Because we do not want the beetle to be visible on the starting back- drop. Then, when the beetle receives the message, "Start Game," it will show itself. Remember the START button? That was its job: to transmit the "Start Game" message.

The last script (previous page; far right) is simply to hide the beetle when the "Game Over" message is received. We haven't coded that part yet, but you can still add it in preparation for the future.

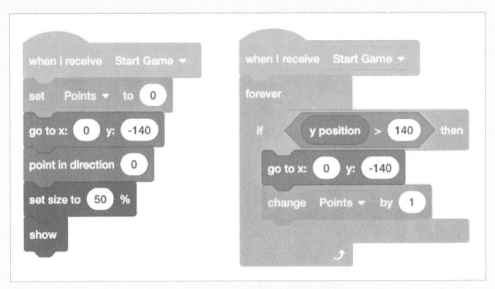

Next, the beetle has two scripts that begin running when it receives the "Start Game" message.

The left-side script positions the beetle at the bottom of the screen and resets any adjustments in points, point in direction, or size that may have occurred in earlier game play.

The right-side script is an IF-THEN block (see page 39 for more on this). It is waiting for the beetle to reach the top of the stage, which I wrote as (y position > 140). I chose 140 rather than the top of the screen (180) because I found that the beetle never actually reaches the top of the stage, and therefore, using a smaller number like 140 was a better choice. Once the beetle reaches the other side of the road, it will have a y position greater than 140, so it will be sent back to the other side of the road (y:-140).

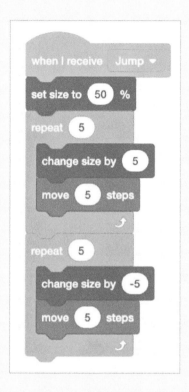

Jump! Jump, little beetle, your life depends on it!

You'll need to add a script that listens for the broadcast "Jump." This script looks a little confusing, so let me break it down for you.

First, the script sets the size of the beetle to 50%. This is to fix a bug (a programming bug, not our beetle!) that is caused if you click the JUMP button really quickly (the beetle will keep growing in size).

Next, do you see those two REPEAT blocks? They both do the same thing, but one increases the beetle's size and the other reduces the beetle's size. Why would we do this? Because it creates the illusion of the beetle jumping on the stage. When the size increases, the beetle appears closer, and when the size decreases, she looks like she's farther away.

Therefore, if the script is coded correctly, the beetle should hop across the road with each click of the JUMP button.

CONVERTIBLE CAR

Convertible 2

Cars are fast and dangerous to beetles crossing the road. And these cars are not slowing down for any beetles in their way! I chose "Convertible 2" for this game.

Just like the beetle sprite, we will need to hide the car at the beginning of the game, since the "Start" backdrop will be showing.

Then, when the car receives the "Start Game" message, it will begin creating clones of itself. To make the game a little more fun, I added a PICK RANDOM block to make the cars appear at random times.

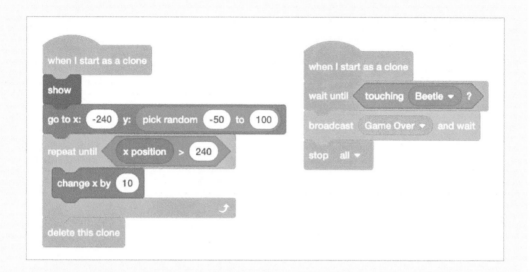

Clones only listen to events that begin with WHEN I START AS A CLONE. For the car sprite, you will need two clone event scripts.

The left-side clone script positions the car on the left side of the screen, but at a random y position between -50 and 100. Then, the car will move, thanks to the CHANGE X BY 10 block, until it reaches the far right-side edge, which is the x position of 240 on the stage. Once the edge is reached, the clone will delete itself.

TESTING THE GAME

I know, that was a lot of code to build a pretty simple game, wasn't it? But hopefully it was worth the effort, and kids are lining up around the block to play your game! So click the start flag and let's see if everything works! The cars should drive on the road and the player should be able to make the beetle jump across. The game ends if the beetle doesn't cross the road without hitting a car.

DELETE THE CLONE

In our game, the cars are clones. If you forget to add the line of code to "delete this clone" when it reaches the far right-side of the screen, then clones will fill up the stage, until there are so many that it finally causes errors as the computer runs out of memory to process all of the clones.

DON'T REPEAT YOURSELF (DRY)

Coders like to keep their code as simple as possible, and they hate to write the same code twice. We call this DRY coding (Don't Repeat Yourself). As a programmer, you should always look for ways to simplify and reorganize your code.

TRY THESE CODING CHALLENGES

1. Customize the look of this game with your own original backdrops.
2. Add different car costumes.
3. Make some cars drive from right to left.
4. Give the beetle three lives before "Game Over."
5. The game does not have a "You Win!" scenario. Add the ability to win the game.
6. Create different backdrops and switch them every time the beetle crosses the road.

TENNIS PONG

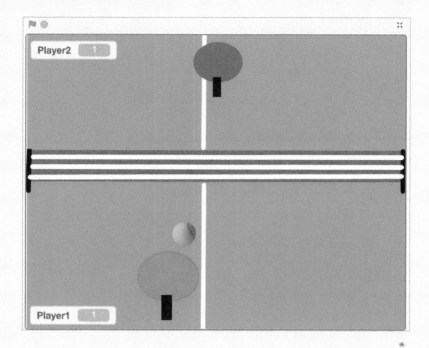

Are you ready for the ultimate table tennis challenge? In our action-packed game, you'll be battling for points against the computer. Yes, your computer will be Player 2 in this modern version of the classic arcade game Pong.

WHAT YOU'LL LEARN

1. Booleans
2. Computer-controlled Player 2

BEFORE YOU BEGIN

1. Create variables named "Player1," "Player2," and "Start." If you need a refresher on how to create a variable, see page 46.
2. Paint a backdrop of a ping-pong table. If you need help with painting backdrops, see page 37.
3. Add the sprite "Tennis Ball" from the sprite library, and draw the "Player1" and "Player2" paddles before coding, since these sprites need to be available in the drop-down selectors prior to coding. Look ahead in the chapter to find these sprites.

RECIPE

I'm a fan of the classic game Pong. It was one of the first video games. I thought about teaching you how to build basic Pong, but then I realized you might enjoy something a little more modern. I really had fun creating my version of ping-pong, and I hope you have fun building it, as well as playing it.

TENNIS BALL

Tennis Ball

For my game of ping-pong, I am using the "Tennis Ball" sprite from the library.

The code for the ball may look complicated, but it's nothing you haven't already learned. I'm going to break it down and explain each script individually.

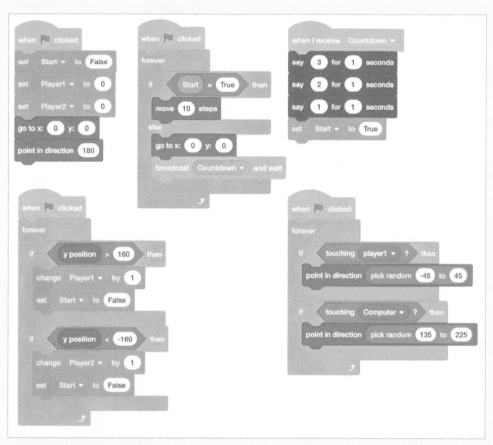

The top-left script is the starting code, which resets all the variables and puts the ball in the center court. But why did I set the variable "Start" to FALSE? I am going to use the "Start" variable to control when the game begins, and I will do this by switching its value from FALSE to TRUE.

The last step of the starting script points the ball in the down direction. If I don't set that direction in the starting script, the ball may move sideways at the start, and since our court goes up and down, we definitely do not want that!

The top-center script is also part of the starting script, but it has a specific job: to restart the game after each point. This script has a conditional (if-then-else) statement that is looking for a TRUE value. If the "Start" variable is TRUE, then the code will move the ball 10 steps. But remember, we set the "Start" variable to FALSE at the beginning of the game. Therefore, the first half of this script will not run at the beginning of the game; only the *else* portion will.

And what does the *else* do? It positions the ball in the center of the stage (x:0, y:0) and broadcasts the message "Countdown." If you need to review how to create a broadcast, see page 60.

The top-right script, "when I receive Countdown," adds some extra professionalism to the game start. I made the tennis ball say "3, 2, 1" before the start variable is changed to TRUE. I think it's a fun way to start the game, but you may want to improve upon it even more!

The bottom-left script controls the score in the game. The conditionals (IF-THEN blocks) are checking to see if the ball moves either above (y:160) or below (y:-160), which will be the edges of the ping-pong table. You'll notice that I didn't use the full height of the stage (y:180), because sprite positions are measured from their center point, and they may not reach the (y:180) position. After increasing the appropriate score, the conditionals (IF-THEN blocks) both change the "Start" variable back to FALSE. Setting the "Start" variable to FALSE triggers the top-center script to reset the ball in the center position for a new volley.

The bottom-right script controls the direction the ball bounces when it hits a player's paddle. We need to use the PICK RANDOM NUMBER block to

CODING FOR KIDS SCRATCH

make the balls bounce in random directions; otherwise, the game would be very boring and predictable. Possibly the trickiest part of this code script is figuring out the direction the ball will bounce after touching the paddle. The direction for Player 1 is actually pretty simple: between -45 and 45. But the direction for Player 2 is much more challenging because we need the ball to point in a downward direction. If you're a math whiz and understand that a circle is 360 degrees, you may be able to figure this out on your own. If not, I suggest following my sample code and using PICK RANDOM 135 TO 225.

PLAYER 1

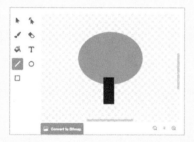

I'm not an artist, but I must admit, my ping-pong paddle looks pretty nice. I don't really have any secret to my artistic talent, other than drawing a circle with a handle.

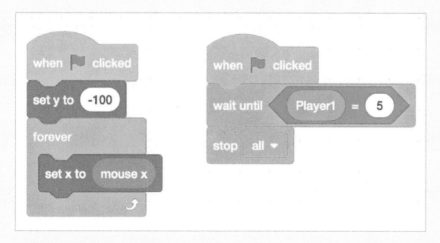

THE GAMES

The code for the Player 1 sprite is superduper easy, compared with the code for the tennis ball! The first script simply positions the paddle on the bottom of the stage (y:-100) and sets the x position to the mouse's x position so the paddle will move left-right to follow your mouse movements.

The second script is a WAIT UNTIL block that will wait until the Player 1 score reaches 5 points before stopping the game.

COMPUTER (PLAYER 2)

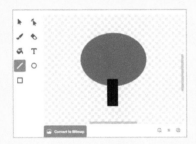

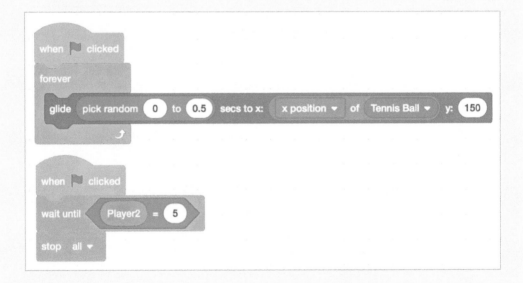

CODING FOR KIDS SCRATCH

Believe it or not, the Player 2 ping-pong paddle is just a copy of the Player 1 paddle, and I simply changed the color to purple. I know, it's beautiful. Should I sell my artwork? What? Not convinced?

Okay, let's get back to creating artificial intelligence. What? Did you just say artificial intelligence? That's awesome! Are we building a robot brain?

Um, actually not a robot brain. Our Player 2's intelligence is going to be pretty simple: just follow the ball's x position. But trust me, it works pretty well.

The secret is to make Player 2 follow the x position of the ball but with a slightly delayed glide speed. Basically, we are intentionally slowing down the computer so we have a chance to win. Why? Because if we didn't slow the computer down, it would always win, every single time! Don't believe me? Okay, then try it with a 0-second delay and see what happens!

You can use any amount of delay to slow down the computer, but I recommend using a PICK RANDOM 0 TO 0.5 block because that seems to work really well. But I'm not a game-playing champion, so it's really up to your personal taste.

The bottom script is exactly the same as Player 1's "Game Over" script. It simply waits until Player 2 has 5 points and then ends the game with a STOP ALL block.

You will probably have trouble finding the "x position of Tennis Ball" block. Don't worry, I'll show you where it is hidden!

In the Block palette, the block is actually called "backdrop # of Stage," and it is found in the Sensing category. To convert the block into "x position of Tennis Ball," you must first change the "Stage" drop-down to "Tennis Ball." Once you make that change, the block will convert into what you needed. Yes, that was a little tricky!

TESTING THE GAME

When you begin the Tennis Pong game, the ball should start in the center of the stage, and then it should say, "3, 2, 1." Then, it should move in a downward direction until the Player 1 paddle touches it. If the paddle touches, the ball will move upward towards the Player 2 paddle. The Player 2 paddle is controlled by the computer, and the computer should be pretty smart about hitting the ball back to you. If either player doesn't touch the ball before it passes by, a point is earned by the other player and the ball is reset to the center position. Game play is over when a player reaches 5 points.

TIPS AND TRICKS

BOOLEANS

Variables that have a value of TRUE or FALSE are known as Booleans in computer coding.

CREATE DEPTH TO YOUR GAME (3D)

You can create depth perception by increasing the size of a sprite when it's closer and decreasing the size when it's farther from you (see Beetle Road on page 126 to learn how it's done).

TRY THESE CODING CHALLENGES

1. Make the ball move slower or faster.
2. Make the ball spin in the air.
3. Let Player 1 choose the skill level of the computer: basic, intermediate, or advanced.

PUTTING IT ALL TOGETHER

Congratulations on becoming a *Scratcher*! Now that you've reached the end of this book, you should feel comfortable with all of the basic coding fundamentals in Scratch. And maybe you've even started sharing some of your games for the world to play!

I hope you can see just how easy and fun it can be to code in Scratch. Sure, there were challenges, and you probably had to fix some bugs along the way. But you've got to admit, Scratch is pretty user-friendly, right?

Just because Scratch is easy to understand doesn't mean you can't make some really professional games. The games you made were terrific starters, but Scratch has also been used in really complex ways. So don't stop here—see where it takes you!

In fact, if you enjoyed building video games with Scratch and you're excited to take the next steps towards becoming a professional coder, you might want to begin learning additional coding languages. Here are some of my suggestions.

HTML is the coding language used to build websites. Coders who build websites are known as web developers. HTML is fun and easy to learn. With just a little practice, you can code and launch your own unique websites to the web.

JavaScript is a coding language used to build complex websites. JavaScript works with HTML to make websites more interactive and even feel a little bit like a video game. If you enjoyed building with Scratch, you might love JavaScript. Why? Because Scratch was built with JavaScript!

Python is a coding language used for creating games, applications, and even search engines. Programmers use Python when they need fast, powerful code to build amazing computer programs. If you have ever used Google or YouTube, you've experienced the power of Python.

Unity is a game engine used to create professional video games on PlayStation, Xbox, Steam, and many other platforms. Game engines are not coding languages; they are a complete system for building games. Game engines work with a variety of coding languages. Unity allows you to build with either JavaScript or C#. Coders who master using a game engine are known as game developers.

So how do you begin learning these other languages? Well, I've put together a list of popular resources in the next section to help you on your journey. You can also search for coding classes near you at this website: code.org/learn/local.

Lastly, don't forget to look me up in the Scratch community page (my user name is HACKINGTONS). And I can't wait to see what you share in the showcase—I know you'll make me proud!

GLOSSARY

Some of these terms were introduced in this book, and others you will discover as you explore Scratch more deeply and continue your coding adventure.

animation: when a collection of similar images are flipped through quickly to trick your eye into seeing movement

backdrop: the image in the game background; it has its own code scripts but cannot have motion blocks

backpack: a storage area on the bottom of the Scratch editor used to save scripts so they can be accessed in other games

binary: a system of two symbols that the computer uses as its language

blocks: individual pieces of code that snap together to give an instruction to the computer; also called code blocks

Boolean: a value of either TRUE or FALSE

bug: an unexpected behavior or error in code

clone: a copy of a sprite

cloud variables: variables that hold information beyond the end of a game; a privilege given to Scratchers in good standing with the Scratch team

coding: writing words a computer will understand; writing code

conditional statement: uses the IF-THEN block to determine if the enclosed code will run or not

conditionals: code blocks that run only if specific conditions are TRUE

costume: a tool that alters the appearance of a sprite

curator: a person who manages a studio of games inside the Scratch website

drag-n-drop: coding that doesn't require typing and moves objects with a mouse

event: triggers a script to begin; common events are WHEN GREEN FLAG CLICKED and WHEN THIS SPRITE CLICKED

library: collection of images or sounds available inside the Scratch program

looks: blocks that can alter a sprite's colors, shape, and visibility

loop: a code block from the control menu that causes code to repeat

messaging: allows sprites to send messages/broadcasts to another sprite; the "listening" sprite will often trigger an Event when it receives the message

motion: blocks that control movement

my blocks: advanced customizable code blocks primarily used for organizing complex scripts that have advanced features like running without screen refresh and multiple input parameters

operators: blocks used for mathematical operations that act as conditional inputs for IF-THEN blocks; can hold values of numbers, Booleans, and letters

pixels: very small colored dots that make up the images on the computer screen

project: a game (finished or unfinished) in Scratch

prototype: an early model of an idea

random numbers: used in video games to create unpredictability of events or movement

run: to start a coding script

Scratcher: experienced Scratch coder

script: when Scratch code blocks are snapped together to form instructions for a sprite to follow

shared: projects that can be seen, played, and remixed by others

sprites: the main images or characters in a video game (not including the backdrop)

stage: the window in which the video game is played

studio: a collection of games that are shared to the public

unshare: to make a game private and not visible to the public

variable: a custom-made code block that can be named and assigned a value

RESOURCES

For more about this book, visit Hackingtons.com/CodingForKids.

I've created a working prototype of each game in this book so you can compare it with your own. Sometimes Scratch project website addresses can change, so always check back to the Hackingtons website for an updated version of the games. This can help you see how the finished product works—yours may look quite different, and that's a good thing!

Cake Clicker: Scratch.MIT.edu/projects/277403472
Late for School!: Scratch.MIT.edu/projects/284855021
Dino Hunt: Scratch.MIT.edu/projects/277417025
Cat and Mouse Chase: Scratch.MIT.edu/projects/282120661
Scuba Adventure: Scratch.MIT.edu/projects/277412885
Balloon Pop!: Scratch.MIT.edu/projects/277522122
Space Jumper: Scratch.MIT.edu/projects/277515547
Crystal Keeper: Scratch.MIT.edu/projects/277846933
Beetle Road: Scratch.MIT.edu/projects/277848177
Tennis Pong: Scratch.MIT.edu/projects/276757256

For Adults and Educators
Scratch information for parents: Scratch.MIT.edu/parents
Scratch resources for teachers: Scratch.MIT.edu/educators
ScratchED (online community for educators):
   ScratchED.gse.harvard.edu

Google CS First (free computer science curriculum):
   CSFirst.WithGoogle.com/s/en/home
Scratch Wiki:
   en.Scratch-Wiki.info/wiki/Scratch_Wiki

Online Tutorials, Coding Lessons, and More Coding Adventures
Hackingtons (classroom and online coding lessons for kids):
   Hackingtons.com
Code.org (free coding lessons for kids and educators): Code.org
w3schools (HTML, JavaScript, and Python): w3schools.com
Codecademy (HTML, JavaScript, and Python): Codecademy.com
Unity Lessons (Unity game development): Unity3D.com/learn
MIT App Inventor (app coding from the makers of Scratch):
   APPInventor.MIT.edu/explore
Micro:bit (microcomputers coded with Scratch blocks): Microbit.org

RESOURCES

INDEX

INDEX

ACKNOWLEDGMENTS

I'd like to thank the Lifelong Kindergarten group at MIT Media Lab for creating and maintaining Scratch.

My wife and kids, for supporting me throughout my journey as both an entrepreneur and author.

The staff and kids at Hackingtons, for laughing at (most) of my jokes.

And the wonderful team at Callisto Media for making this book possible.

ABOUT THE AUTHOR

Matthew Highland lives in the East Bay area of California, near San Francisco. Along with his cofounder Steven Croft and a great team of teachers and staff, he creates curriculum for Hackingtons Code School for Kids.

When he is not busy with CEO stuff, Matthew loves skateboarding with his son Jack and fishing with his son Maxwell.

Matthew started his teaching career in Tokyo, Japan. He often travels to Japan with his family. Matthew's wife, Hiromi, was born and raised on a small island in the Sea of Japan named Shōdoshima, so, of course, his family visits Shōdoshima, where they eat lots and lots of sushi!

Matthew's Scratch username is HACKINGTONS. Feel free to say hello or check out some of his projects in the showcase!